Wanderlust
and lipstick

for Women Traveling to India

Wanderlust
and lipstick
for Women Traveling to India

Beth Whitman

DISPATCH
travels

PO Box 16102
Seattle WA 98116
www.dispatchtravels.com

Wanderlust and Lipstick: For Women Traveling to India

© 2008 by Beth Whitman

Published by:
Dispatch Travels
PO Box 16102
Seattle, WA 98116

ISBN 10: 0978728084
ISBN 13: 9780978728083

Editor: Amy Scott
Illustrations: Elizabeth Haidle

LCCN: 2008905674

Purchase additional copies online at:
www.WanderlustAndLipstick.com

Printed in the U.S.A.

CONTENTS

PREFACE

The saying goes that you either love India or you have it. Yet after my first trip there nearly two decades ago, I came away feeling quite neutral — without a strong desire to return but not disliking the country. I suppose my Wanderlust runs far too deep to cross any country off of my travel list.

Living in Seattle, I have the good fortune to be centered in one of the hubs of technology, which has drawn people from around the globe, including India. I have many friends from the subcontinent. And while we have snickered over the years about the realities of India — the likelihood of stepping in cow poop, the tenacious touts who all but beg for your business, the immense poverty that cannot be avoided and the buses that break down in remote villages — my faded memories were based on a single trip in my early 20s.

What I have observed in these friends is that they are inextricably linked by warm and gentle spirits...a kindness that permeates from their karmic cores. It's because of my friends in the U.S. that I felt the pull to return to India. Some of these friends had moved back to their home country, giving Jon, my significant other, and me an instant safety net and friendly faces to visit. Others had family still living in India. All of them opened their homes, hearts and kitchens(!) to us — and again to me on a subsequent solo trip.

Now, my nose is pierced; my tea cupboard is filled with chai; my spice rack spills over with *sambar,* fennel and turmeric; and sitar music and incense are never far away when I want to be lulled back to Mother India.

So many people participate in the creation of a book. I thank all of the women whom I interviewed and who freely shared their experiences and love for India. I learned a tremendous amount from these strong and thoughtful wanderers. I also thank Amy Scott, my editor, whose guidance and knowledge of India was invaluable and helped shape what you are holding. Claudia Smelser designed the cover and interior layout and wasn't afraid to push the boundaries of either. Beth Haidle, my illustrator, produced another set of kick-ass illustrations for each chapter. I can't help but smile every time I flip through the book and see these unique drawings. The support that I receive from Jon is ineffable. He is my pillar, my sounding board, my reality check.

Above all, however, I owe thanks to Mother India herself. Thank you for showing me that even in the midst of complete chaos, there is the possibility for peace of mind. Thanks for magnifying my belief that what you give is what you get. Your shining example taught me that when you have faith, karmic law will always show you the way.

Beth Whitman
2008

BEFORE YOU READ ON

As you read through this guide *For Women Traveling to India,* keep a few things in mind.

All costs are quoted in U.S. dollars unless otherwise noted.

The information in this book is pulled from my experiences as an avid traveler to India and includes opinions and quotes from other women who have traveled throughout the country. Travel is a personal matter and we all bring our own prejudices and backgrounds to our experiences. You may not agree with all that I have to say but I hope that you'll use this guide as a primer to get you started and excited to plan your journey.

Writing one book about India is like trying to see and understand the entire country over a long weekend. It's impossible. If you feel I've missed something critical to making a woman's journey to the subcontinent more of a success, please let me know — I'm always open to learning!

There are a vast number of companies providing information, services and products to the travel industry that benefit travelers to India that did not make it into this first edition of *Wanderlust and Lipstick: For Women Traveling to India.* In the interest of space and time, I have included those companies for which I have a strong favorable opinion and those that offer a unique service. If you feel that I've missed something important, please send me an email.

While every possible effort has been made to include correct company and website information, it's not uncommon for URLs to change or for companies to change their names or go out of business. If you see a listing that you believe is incorrect, please let me know.

Finally, travel information about India and beyond is always fresh and fun on my website, www.WanderlustAndLipstick. com. Come peruse, learn and share!

Thanks!

Beth

beth@WanderlustAndLipstick.com

1.

EMERGING INDIA

I FIRST *traveled to India in 1989. As a young backpacker, I was overwhelmed by the difficulty of maneuvering around the subcontinent — booking train tickets took an act of god(s), cashing a travelers check was a three-hour process at a hard-to-locate bank, and finding a restaurant that would serve me (as a woman) at the same time as my traveling companion (a man) was rare — men were always served first. Things are changing.*

Many years later India finds herself in the process of explosive growth as a technology hub, as a country on the cutting edge of medical advances and as a popular tourist destination. A developing country? Absolutely! But far more advanced now than one might initially imagine.

Today, traveling from Delhi to Bangalore is as easy as booking (online) a low-cost airline ticket; rupees can be obtained at an ATM machine in seconds; and good, healthy, inexpensive and well-served meals can be found in any city or village that hosts even a minimal amount of tourist traffic.

India is starting to attract more backpackers, businesspeople, tour groups and luxury travelers. But given its size and population relative to these visitors there are still tremendous opportunities to discover quiet beaches, be part of a small group discovering the wonders of a safari park and visit villages in which few (if any) tourists have ever set foot.

Add to this a dash of political stability and economic strength, and you've got the makings for a country well worth a visit (or two or three or four!).

↩Incredible India

The Indian government recognized that other Asian countries (namely Thailand, Singapore and China) were attracting millions more tourists each year than its own country. In response, they brilliantly launched the Incredible India campaign in the wake of September 11th. Luring travelers with beautiful photos and the promise of "a path to *ananda*" (wellness, bliss and contentment), the campaign has dramatically helped increase foreign tourism. According to the Ministry of Tourism website (www.tourism.gov.in), the number of travelers to India rose from approximately 3.5 million visitors in 2004 to an estimated five million in 2007.

India has responded in kind to this growth. The government has launched campaigns to train those in the tourism industry (from taxi drivers to customs officials) about hygiene, appropriate conduct, politeness and integrity (including charging fair prices!) as well as safety and security. Anticipating that the demand for hotel rooms will, and in some cities already has, outpaced supply, the Ministry of Tourism is encouraging locals to convert their homes into bed-and-breakfasts.

For better or worse, restaurants, cafés, shopping malls and full-on grocery stores are cropping up in cities and in the countryside. Although the traffic and pollution can be stifling, Delhi and Kolkata have built elevated railway systems that help improve air quality and reduce commute times.

Though backpackers have long been aware of India's treasures, from beaches to temples, middle- to high-income travelers are just now discovering the subcontinent. Travel has become easier and friendlier, luring even those who don't consider themselves adventurous.

Bangalore and Hyderabad are now home to offices for companies such as Microsoft, Yahoo!, AOL, Google and Amazon. Indians who left for greener pastures now find it possible to return to an India in which the infrastructure is beginning to stabilize and where modern amenities are now available. Returning "home," they have begun to have children and are enjoying support from their families and servants (which they can easily afford in India).

But all is not sunny…

The country is still enough of a challenge to make it interesting. Alexandra, a masters student from Brighton, England, spent eight months there. "I loved the absolute insaneness of it all. It took everything I knew and could relate to and threw it out the window. I saw the most beautiful and breathtaking things, then, in the same instant, the most horrific images."

India is indeed a land of extremes. Bangalore, once the "pensioner's paradise," has grown so rapidly that it's renowned for having the worst traffic in India. You could call it the California of the subcontinent. Slums abound in and around every major city, while the wealthy own the most extravagant of homes and employ many servants.

Population growth has caused an increase in the pollution level and resulting death toll in Delhi even though the city had enjoyed a slight dip in smog a decade ago. Water is in short supply in much of the country and the land is being stripped of its nutrients.

In addition to these problems that result from overpopulation, other issues make India a test for visitors. Sectarian bombings occur on occasion, a result of the ongoing rift between Hindus and Muslims. Religious sites and holy cities can be targets, and random train and market bombings are not uncommon, but they don't happen frequently enough to warrant canceling your trip.

For the woman Wanderluster, there is the challenge of dealing with incessant stares from men and their attempts at catching your attention with their ongoing remarks including, "Madame, Madame, you buy? Please come see my jewelry shop. You need hotel? Rickshaw, Madame?" Under these circumstances, all you can think is, "Serenity now!"

Don't let India's early stages of tourism, nor its challenges, steer you elsewhere, however. This is an exciting period in India's history, and there's never been a better time to visit.

FOLLOW YOUR PASSIONS

WITH *more than one billion people, India boasts hundreds of languages, 600 tribal groups, a deeply religious psyche, a growing economy and a prolific arts community that includes Bollywood and traditional and modern music. It's impossible to experience it all in one trip. Instead, home in on your specific area(s) of interest and experience the country in small, digestible amounts, based on your hobbies and passions.*

⤳ Culture

Festivals — Many people travel to India specifically to attend a festival or major religious event. These occur virtually year-round. Many began as either religious celebrations or a way to bless the harvest season; now they often incorporate both.

These festivals are vibrant and colorful occasions that bring together communities. While you're sure to stumble upon celebrations along the way, there are some that are worth scheduling your trip to attend. Note that festivals are based on the lunar calendar, so the actual dates change yearly.

Diwali is the festival of lights and arguably one of the most visually beautiful of India's celebrations because of all the brilliant lamps and bulbs lighting up cities and villages. *Diwali* falls sometime between mid-October and mid-November and signifies the triumph of good over evil.

Holi is the festival of color and is celebrated in February or March. Both colored powder and water are liberally thrown at friends and strangers alike, all in good fun. Its roots are based upon the myth that Lord Krishna applied color to Radha's cheek because she was so fair-skinned. Now all get to join in!

Kaydin, from British Columbia, spent a year in India as part of a Rotary International exchange program and was fortunate to have been in India during a festival. "*Holi* is about friends and fun. Beforehand you drink *thandai,* which is made from cashew milk and includes marijuana. You then smear color over everyone. It's mixed with water and everyone's clothes get ridiculously covered."

Kumbh Mela is a Hindu pilgrimage that occurs every four years at various religious sites around the country. A *maha* (great) *Kumbh Mela* occurs every 12 years; millions attend, making it the greatest gathering of humans anywhere. As many as 70 million were reportedly present at the 2007 event in Allahabad.

Pushkar Camel Fair is held every November in Rajasthan. Thousands of foreign visitors compete for tent space with the camel traders that come from around the country to bargain and barter.

Hot Tip! Festival time is popular for Indians living in-country and abroad. Book flights and hotels early if you plan to attend one of these festivals. Treat this as a way to get to know the locals and the r customs by asking questions and joining in the celebrations.

Sankrathi is in January and is celebrated differently throughout the country. Homes may be marked by chalk drawings at the doorstep and family members and neighbors may exchange gifts. Villages swell with pilgrims and street performers entertain all.

Film — The first time I saw a Hindi film, I was traveling by (local) bus on my way to Varanasi many moons ago. I shook my young head in absolute astonishment that Indians actually enjoyed the unlikely outbursts of singing, dancing and shimmying that was peppered with simple dialogue.

Many years later I now find these films endearing and seek them out. I regularly rent them from Netflix (www.netflix.com) at home and attend the cinema when I'm in India (without subtitles).

Now that I understand the culture better, it no longer surprises me that Indians love these movies. After a day of honking horns, blowing dust, intense traffic and the constant reminder of the poverty that fills the country, who wouldn't love to tuck away into a dark movie theater for less than a dollar and be

2. FOLLOW YOUR PASSIONS

diverted by romance, music, dancing and sweeping panoramic views of the Kashmiri mountains (though the movies are now filmed in Switzerland and other European countries due to unrest in Kashmir).

Bollywood, whose home is Mumbai (formerly Bombay) is a large slice of the film-industry pie, but film buffs may already know that the Indian film industry reaches far wider. All in all, India churns out the largest number of films worldwide each year and sells more tickets than any other country.

It's easy to find movie houses in every city, including cinemas that are cropping up in Western-style malls, and Indian films are shown regularly on satellite television channels. According to the Central Board of Film Certification in Mumbai (www.cbfcindia.tn.nic.in), more than a billion people (India's population) go to the cinema every three months. That's an astounding number!

Even though many of the films are shown in a hybrid mix of Hindi and English (Hinglish) without subtitles, you can easily enjoy the experience since attending a movie is not just about the film. You'll be surrounded by babies wailing, couples snuggling and talking, and cell phones ringing, all overpowering the soundtrack at times. Expect an intermission for snacks and a toilet break.

Hot Tip! If you attend a movie in a tiered theater, sit in the most expensive seats and try to sit next to other women or a couple. There have been reports of women being harassed if not accompanied by a male. Don't encourage attempts at conversation from interested men.

You may have an opportunity to make your film debut in a Bollywood flick. Advertisements in city newspapers, particularly in Mumbai, list opportunities for foreigners to earn a few dollars (and I mean a few) by joining the cast and crew for a day of shooting. One traveler I met said he was approached at a train station and immediately jumped at the chance to take part. A day of shooting may be long and it's doubtful you'll get to meet Bollywood stars SRK or Aishwarya Rai, but what an experience to write home about!

Music — While driving from Varkala to Trivandrum with my travel buddy, Kate, our taxi driver, who was definitely pushing 60, cranked up the radio. With a Hindi pop tune blaring from the speakers, he began snapping his fingers and jerking his head back and forth while he checked the rearview mirror to make sure we were enjoying his performance.

I listen to world music almost exclusively when I'm at home. Therefore, any time I travel, I make a beeline to the closest CD or musical instrument store.

Music also plays a prominent role in the lives of all Indians. Whether it's pop music extracted from Bollywood flicks or classical ragas, there's no shortage of ear candy coming from cars, buses, trucks, restaurants, retail shops and even mobile phones.

With so many filmgoers, soundtracks are an easy way for artists to reach a wide audience really quickly. Stay in the country for more than a couple of weeks and you'll recognize the same songs being played over and over on the radio and at wedding processions that roam the streets. The popularity of these songs fades just as quickly as it arises — if you're in search of a favorite song, get to a store quickly to catch it while it's still available.

Of course, India's music scene isn't all about popular culture. Classical music has a wide-reaching audience as well. Generally played on a sitar (a stringed instrument made famous in the West by Ravi Shankar) and tabla (drum), this ancient art form may have a singer accompanying the instruments. Restaurants may provide a free evening of entertainment featuring classical musicians.

Think of all this music as your personal soundtrack to India, ever-changing with the landscape and situation.

Hot Tip! Pick up a few CDs before heading home. They're cheap and lightweight, making great souvenirs or gifts.

Painting — Few places provide artists with as much visual stimulation as India. Whether you are traveling to be inspired by the country itself or by other artists, you'll have plenty to draw upon.

Various distinct styles of painting have developed throughout India. The art was originally influenced by religion and by the rich who funded the arts, namely those of the Raj and Mughal eras.

Fascinated by the culture, Connie studied Indian art at Smith College. "It's easier to understand the art after studying the various religions of India and reading the accompanying primary sources like the Vedas, the Upanishads and the Bhagavad Gita. Having this overview then makes it easier to focus on specific periods of art."

For help in deciphering the variety of painting styles, visit museums in the larger cities where excellent collections have been procured to demonstrate the difference in styles over time.

While traveling with a group of artists, Carolyn visited many studios and was always well received by the locals. "The Indians warmed up to us because we had something in common. We were able to talk the same language."

Dance — Watching one Indian film should be enough for you to realize that Indians *love* their dance. The shimmying, shaking shoulders of India's best actors make locals and visitors alike want to jump in — it's that infectious. But, like music, Bollywood-influenced dance is not the only style you'll see across the subcontinent.

Traditional and folk styles are also prevalent. Many emerged as part of religious ceremonies and are now performed as entertainment or as part of rituals such as festivals or weddings.

The entertainment sections of local newspapers and *Time Out* magazines (www.timeout.com) will list performances at major concert halls and venues. Smaller villages that draw lots of tourists may also have nightly performances scheduled specifically for visitors. Examples of the types of dance you might see include *Kathakali* in Kerala, *Odissi* in Orissa and *Bharatanatyam* in Tamil Nadu.

Dance classes are available in schools that offer both private and group instruction. In addition to traditional Indian dance, you can also learn Latin, tap or jazz.

Architecture — You could easily spend a year in India visiting great architectural marvels. While the Taj Mahal stands out as the finest example in the country, arguably in the world, the country is filled with buildings and structures worth a visit.

Religious architecture dominates every village and city and includes temples, statues, mosques, mausoleums and stupas, often incorporating detailed sculptures. Each style draws upon ancient and revered designs that have evolved over the centuries and that have absorbed influences from other cultures.

Many are UNESCO World Heritage Sites, such as the ancient temple of Hampi and the erotically sculpted temple in Khajuraho.

With a special appreciation of the artistic work in these buildings, Connie said, "I'm amazed by the attention to detail and the religious expression that comes through in the temples as the embodiment of the deity."

Magnificent palaces and forts, symbols of wealth and protecting that wealth, dominate the architectural landscape but are most concentrated in the Mughal-influenced region of Rajasthan.

✿ Religion

I sat in a café on a busy street in Kolkata waiting for the camera hospital (that's what the sign said) to open so that I could retrieve my sick Canon. As I sat sipping my coffee with milk, I watched people pass by this open-aired coffee shop and pause to say a prayer to the Ganesh poster that hung in the doorway.

Religion permeates every aspect of life in India. Rituals are openly practiced without shame or shyness and are not reserved for a special day of the week. Instead, religion is part of life and prayers are offered several times each day during *puja* (meditation or calls to prayer).

India was part of a round-the-world trip for Quinnette. She noticed this same behavior during the India portion of her journey. "As a traveler, you are sort of a voyeur. People are doing their sacred things every day."

But you don't have to be just a voyeur. Many travel to India explicitly to meet a guru or to study a particular religion, meditation or yoga practice.

Sigrid is an avid traveler and belongs to a loosely knit group in Seattle called the Wayward Women. She believes that it's this all-encompassing atmosphere that gives Indians their tolerance. "Because of their religion, they are very respectful. They allow people to just be. You see an allowance of things when you see the streets filled with cows and people. As people become more Western, they lose some of that allowance."

Courtney was in India for two and a half months and during that time visited the Golden Temple in Amritsar during the birthday of Guru Nanek (the founder of the Sikh religion). "We were coming out of the temple and this Sikh man from Canada started telling us all about Sikhism. I was skeptical at first — there are many people who offer things who have an agenda. But he wanted to take us on a tour where we got to see the back rooms where they make the dough for chapattis. He wanted us to know everything about Sikhism."

What Courtney learned was that shortly after September 11th there was a concentrated effort in the United States and abroad to inform people about Sikhs so there wouldn't be so much prejudice against them. This man was acting as an ambassador for that cause.

It's difficult to return home without having observed or participated in at least some ritual, as it is so firmly implanted in the arts, dance, education, politics, architecture and food.

❧ Volunteer

Whether volunteering is the sole purpose of your journey or is a component of a longer trip, you're sure to be able to offer a tremendous amount of help in one of two ways.

For shorter trips, consider joining a *humanitour*, in which humanitarian opportunities are an integral part of the trip. This

༄༄༄ Alexandra's Story ༄༄༄

I volunteered in a very small village in Kerala called Vazhakulam, which is about two and a half hours east of Cochin. It was very rural and I felt as though many of the locals had never set eyes on white skin before. It was me and another girl from England who were staying with a local family. We had our own room and washroom.

My friend and I were quite the spectacle. Every time we left the house it was as if the circus came to town. We taught Monday through Friday during regular school hours to children between the ages of 10 and 17.

In McLeod Ganj, I volunteered for six weeks with Volunteer Tibet (www.volunteertibet.org), a nonprofit organization that does community work with Tibetan refugees. I was teaching three women English as well as doing social activities with them. A lot of the refugees have no family or friends when they arrive so the organization loves for you to be involved with the students socially and on a more personal level. The three women I was working with were seamstresses. I taught four to five times a week at their work or in one of their homes.

I found Volunteer Tibet on the Internet. I learned about the organization and then just showed up in person and was placed.

will give you a combination of sightseeing and volunteering in order to experience the culture up close. Examples are volunteering at an orphanage, ashram, temple or school.

For longer stays, consider working with a nongovernmental organization and spending a longer period of time strictly working within a volunteer environment. Programs range in length from days to one year.

Simone worked with Habitat for Humanity for two weeks in a small village north of Chennai. Even though this was an organized program, she found that there were many other ways to help that were equally as important.

"Even if you're in India for a short time, you can give to poor communities by bringing pens and paper with you that can be purchased in the bigger cities, such as Delhi or Mumbai," she said. "Also, schools would be happy to have a foreigner come in just to do a lesson. There are always people who want to just practice their English."

∿ Photography

Whether you're a budding amateur or professional photographer, there will be ample opportunity to photograph fascinating people, cultural activities, exciting festivals, colorful clothing and bustling markets.

Be honest with yourself about how committed you are to taking pictures and decide accordingly how much and which equipment you want to carry with you. Cameras can be cumbersome, particularly film cameras with all the accompanying film. The potential of having a camera stolen and of regularly having to backup your digital images may also factor into your decision.

Once you've decided what camera you'll be bringing, pore over coffee-table photography books of India. These help me determine not only which cities or villages I'd like to visit but also what I'd like to photograph once I'm there.

Take a photography class prior to your trip and you'll see an improvement in your pictures compared to past journeys. Check community centers and local colleges for evening and weekend classes taught by experienced photographers or take a tour to India that focuses on photography and is led by a professional in the field.

There is usually an additional charge for bringing still and video cameras into tourist sights and photography is forbidden at military installations, airports and even some tourist attractions (Akshardham Temple in Delhi, for instance).

Not every Indian will be comfortable with having his or her picture taken. If people don't outwardly stop you, their body language may tell you as much (for example, a woman may pull her scarf over her head and face). Respect their wishes and move on.

In addition to a still camera, consider carrying a small video camera, which can record audio as well as people, architecture and landscapes. With my little high-definition video camera, I captured stunning scenery of Kerala's backwaters as the train gently moved along the tracks; I also stood outside of Buddhist temples to record chanting monks.

Hot Tip! You may find yourself in front of the camera as much as behind it. As a foreign woman traveler in India, you'll be an oddity (see Chapter 3, Culture Shock, to read about Western Curiosity) and may be asked to star in many other people's photos. Whether you choose to pose or not, be gracious about the request.

While with a friend in Delhi, Jamie didn't feel threatened but was bothered by constantly being the subject of others' photos. "Two young guys were following us around the Red Fort. They were probably just shy but they kept following us around and taking our pictures. The first time it's funny. The second time it's funny. But after the fifth or sixth time you start to wonder. After that many times, it ceased to be OK with me. It was not only inappropriate, it was also getting to be too much."

↝ Health

Yoga and Meditation — While you may practice yoga or meditation at home, sometimes you just need to get out of your normal routine in order to fine-tune your skills.

The Beatles popularized yoga and meditation in India during the 1960s. Many a hippie and yuppie have followed in their footsteps in the decades since, and the popularity continues.

As the birthplace of yoga, India has an abundance of yoga centers teaching disciplines such as Hatha, Bikram, Pranayama, Iyengar, Siddha, Kundalini, Tantra and more. Regardless of the type, it's likely to be taught differently than its Western counterpart. Before committing with cash down, ask lots of questions of your instructor and the center as the quality of both facility and teacher will vary greatly while you attempt to unite yourself with the divine.

Centers and personal instructors are located throughout India, though some of the more popular concentrations of practitioners are in Rishikesh, Pune, Mysore, Kerala and Goa. While we were in Varkala, Kerala, Kate remarked to me, "You can't walk around here without being able to spit on someone with a yoga mat." It was true. It seemed everyone but me was in this small cliffside village to practice yoga.

I meditated on my coffee and banana pancakes instead.

A yoga teacher herself, Jessica traveled to India specifically to study yoga. "There are more flavors to yoga than there are Baskin Robbins. The one I signed up for was not my style. Even though it was a form of what I study and teach in the U.S., it was too different. I stayed for two days and then found a new teacher."

If you want to take formal yoga classes at a center or ashram, registering in advance is advised as classes fill quickly. However, you may run into the same issue as Jessica, so inquire about their refund policy. Hourly lessons can be taken informally where studios and private teachers are more prevalent such as in the locations listed earlier.

If meditation is your path, search for a center that accommodates your belief system. Some have very strict rules, including participation in silent times or many hours of chanting or, in the case of the Osho Meditation Resort (www.osho.com) in Pune, the requirement to take an HIV/AIDS test prior to entering the facility (even for tours) due to their liberal on-site sexual policy.

Meditation practices in India include Vedanta, Vipassana and Tibetan Buddhist and are generally taught at an ashram. The facility may or may not have a leader or guru and programs range from one week to several months. An online search will result in many options but it's always wise to ask for referrals or check forums. (See Chapter 4, Mapping Out the Details, for forums to visit.)

Ayurveda — This traditional Indian practice is an integrated approach to health based on holistic healing, including the balancing of the *doshas* (body types) through food and herbal remedies. The right balance brings these three body types (*pitta*, *vata* and *kapha*) into alignment, ultimately preventing disease and illness.

Since India is the source for Ayurveda, having begun there about five thousand years ago, there's really no better place to dive in head first to study this ancient system.

It continues to be a part of everyday life for Indians. Foods are combined in a complementary fashion to include a balance of sour, sweet, salty, bitter, pungent and astringent flavors. In order to realign the *doshas* and purge an illness, herbs, spices, fruits, teas and extracts are ingested rather than Western medication.

Kerala is a well-known region for Ayurvedic courses, and training colleges are found throughout India. Many of these courses are specifically for foreigners and can range from one week to one year.

Medical Treatments — Due to rising costs of health care in the West, medical tourism (traveling to receive medical treatment) has become more accepted in recent years. India is one of the leaders of this new phenomenon, catering to foreign tourists in need of hip replacements, knee surgery, dental work, chemotherapy and stem cell treatments.

Though it's normal to have concerns about traveling to a developing country for a (relatively) low-cost procedure, I would have little hesitation going to a developed part of India for medical care if the need arose.

Procedures cost one-tenth (in the case of a crown for your tooth) to one-half (in the case of a hip replacement) the expense in the West, allowing a person to potentially save tens of thousands of dollars. Many of the doctors in India have been trained in the West and the facilities built to accommodate Western tastes.

Lois, a nutritionist from Texas, traveled to India for a double mastectomy. "The procedure in the U.S. would have cost $20,000. In Mumbai, it's less than $3,000 including airfare and a 10-day hospital stay."

Amy had been suffering from Lyme disease for years. During this time she underwent numerous unsuccessful medical procedures in the U.S. at a cost of nearly $150,000. She then discovered a clinic in Delhi that provided embryonic stem cell

2. FOLLOW YOUR PASSIONS

treatment, including that for Lyme disease. After less than two months of treatment, she saw marked improvements in her condition at a fraction of the cost of those that hadn't been working for her in the U.S.

Some treatments simply aren't available in countries other than India due to government restrictions or pressure from the health-care industry in the developed world. I visited the embryonic stem cell clinic in Delhi where Amy was treated. It uses patent-pending technology unavailable elsewhere. I was pleasantly surprised by the modern facility and was floored by the progress of the patients. Quadriplegics of 15 years were walking with support. They were able to feel their lower extremities and control their bladder and bowel movements for the first time since their accidents.

Ask for referrals from former patients and do extensive research into a clinic's background before agreeing to any procedure.

∾ Weddings

I had always wanted to attend an Indian wedding, having been invited to a half dozen or so by friends, but the timing has yet to work out. However, on my second journey to the subcontinent, I arrived during the height of wedding season (January and February) and found that there were ceremonies spilling out into the streets day and night. After being an unofficial guest of countless processions and observing the long, drawn-out ghat-side ceremonies in Udaipur, I no longer feel the need to get my wedding fix through friends!

If you have the chance to go to India specifically for a wedding, take full advantage of the opportunity. These elaborate affairs take place over several days and come complete with white horses, roaming brass bands and traffic jams as hundreds of brightly clothed women in saris follow the groom on horseback while he gallops through the streets to meet up with his new wife.

Women spend hours having their hands and feet elaborately decorated with henna (as on this book's cover) for their wedding day. The henna powder is made from all-natural ingredients and lasts for one to four weeks before it disappears from the skin.

Hot Tip! Because astrologists determine the best days for weddings, ceremonies are often scheduled with little notice. If invited to a wedding in India, expect to have only two to three months to plan your trip.

See Chapter 11, Pack It Up, for ideas on how to dress appropriately. While saris are not generally worn by foreigners on a daily basis, attending a wedding is the perfect opportunity to test one out.

❧ Food

Food has always been an integral part of any adventure abroad. This seems to be the case now more than ever due to shows like Andrew Zimmern's *Bizarre Foods* on the Travel Channel. People are, well, hungry for quality international food. If you can't get a good curry in your neighborhood, why not head off to India to experience it for yourself?

A devout foodie, Mary-Anne loves traveling to India to discover regional specialties. She says, "Shopping at spice markets in Cochin is always a highlight of a trip!" Each region of India prepares food in its own style, and Mary-Anne has some sage advice for first-time travelers to India. "Read about the cultures of each area you will visit. It's the complexity and diversity of each region that makes Indian food so dear to me. And forget fast foods, street foods are my real favorite."

See Chapter 8, Feasting, for more information on food.

Though they are not as well advertised as you might think, it is possible to attend cooking classes in India. I've seen signs posted up in shop windows advertising local programs and an inquiry at a spice shop or at your hotel may turn up a special invitation to someone's home.

✿ Rest and Relaxation

Hordes of travelers take to the magnificent beaches of India each year. India has approximately 4,700 miles of coastline, and there's little competition from the locals for space on these pristine shores, so it's no wonder that sandy vacations are so popular with tourists.

That's not to say that these areas are completely empty. Popular locations like Goa and Kovalam are swarming with backpackers. You'll enjoy these areas if sunbathing, drinking beer and eating lots of seafood are your idea of R&R. But it doesn't take much to get off the beaten path for some real relaxation. Most areas just away from the major tourist towns can provide tranquility.

The more remote you get, however, the more you will find Indian men trying to get a glimpse of some skin. Simone found this slightly annoying during her beach travels with a gal friend. "We didn't want to go where all the tourists were but wanted to do what the locals were doing. As women travelers, we were given a bit too much unwanted attention from the young males. We just wanted to have some girl time and chill out. Going out and swimming in our bathing suits would have put too much attention on us. It's hard to relax when you're given so much attention. After a few days we just wanted to get away."

See Chapter 11, Pack It Up, for more information on dressing conservatively.

❧ Business

❧❧❧ Wendy's Story ❧❧❧

The three days I spent at my company's Bangalore office were fascinating. My co-workers, whom I had previously met only by email, were wonderful about showing me around, getting me a desk and introducing me to their colleagues. I could see how and why the Bangalore office was so productive; the teams worked hard and were far removed from meddling by the San Jose office.

But there was quite a bit of culture shock. A few times, I accidentally left my camera battery charger plugged in when I left for the evening. The next morning, the security guard would be waiting for me at the door with the battery, the charger, the converter and paperwork to fill out confirming that it had all been returned to me. This was so different from the San Jose headquarters where I once left my battery charger plugged in when I was doing a photo shoot. I went back and found it the next day, right where I had left it in the huge conference room, untouched.

The dogs were another shock. In front of the company's Bangalore office was a handsome security guard, dressed in a perfectly pressed beige uniform. (I assumed a holdover from the British occupation.) He had with him a beautiful brown-and-beige German shepherd, also standing at attention so proud. Seven paces away were more dogs, also German shepherds, but these were eating out of a garbage dump.

With so many foreign companies opening offices in India or interested in doing business there, it's quite possible you could find yourself on that next Air India flight to Hyderabad to conduct or attend business meetings for your job. Jump on the opportunity to do so and factor in a little extra time for jet lag and sightseeing.

INFO FOR THE BUSINESS TRAVELER

- Bold, outspoken behavior may well be looked down upon. If you are an assertive woman, tone down your personality in order to have a successful meeting, contract or sale. While this does go against the grain of my Jersey-girl upbringing, I realize that I have to play by other rules when I'm traveling.

- India is a relationship-based country and companies are often family-owned. Your Indian colleague(s) will invariably "know someone" who can help you with whatever your needs are, be it buying a rug, booking a hotel, finding a restaurant or scheduling a service.

- Have patience. This relationship-based way of communicating and decision-making gives you the opportunity to meet lots of people and you could very well make your way through a business transaction being passed from one individual to another. Relationship-building takes time, however, and can slow down the process of getting a deal done.

- India is synonymous with red tape and bureaucracy. While computers are becoming more ubiquitous, don't be surprised if your colleagues document information in large ledgers filled with hand-printed information.

- First impressions are paramount. Wear conservative, professional clothes. Indian businesspeople will dress more formally than those in the West. Think: New York City business suit rather than Seattle business casual.

✌ Wildlife and Safaris

When you think of India, it's usually the Taj Mahal, the mass of humanity or the food that initially comes to mind. But the country is filled with unique opportunities for wildlife viewing beyond the tourist-ridden elephants in Jaipur. With 350 species of mammals and 2,000 species of birds, there's something for everyone.

Unfortunately, due to India's growing population and the demand on resources, many animal species are considered endangered. Protected areas have been created, often set apart as national parks (of which there are about 100), wildlife sanctuaries (numbering about 500), game reserves and biosphere reserves.

You'll obviously need to join a tour in order to take part in a wildlife safari, including a camel trek in the desert. However, you can visit smaller parks and bird sanctuaries on your own and then choose to hire a guide if you like.

✌✌✌ Courtney's Story ✌✌✌

I took a camel safari out of Jaisalmer. To figure out which company to use, I asked around at a couple of hotels to get a sense of what they offered. I then asked other travelers who they had booked with and if they were satisfied. also asked at hotels that didn't offer safaris so they'd be less biased. ·

I asked about bedding and what their philosophy was with regards to being in the desert and leaving trash. If you ask enough, you'll find someone who doesn't just send you out in the desert with 20 teenagers.

It took me longer to do the research than I thought it would. I thought I could breeze into town and find someone quickly, but

I asked a lot of questions and was very happy with the tour company I chose.

The company was really good about environmental awareness. Though there was no recycling, they packed everything up and then left it at a designated point where it would be picked up later.

I loved the camel safari. You don't realize what an onslaught of noise everything is in India. In the desert there isn't that sensory overload. You don't realize it when you're in it, but when it's quiet, you appreciate the silence.

After the safari, I went to Bharatpur Bird Sanctuary and it was amazing. It was one of the coolest places I'd been in India. The area is at the intersection of a migration pattern and the only place where you can see certain types of birds. I saw 40 to 50 species.

I showed up at the gate and there were all these bird guides. Choosing one was total luck of the draw. You then rent bikes and ride around all day. My guide was really knowledgeable and charged only $20 for the day.

∾ Educational Programs

Student Exchanges — Traveling to India on an educational or student exchange program will allow you to experience the country in a unique way. The program you join can act as a sort of safety net in case you have questions or run into any problems. And, because you may very well be staying with a family, this will give you the chance to experience the culture from a unique perspective.

Look for India-bound programs in your own community, including those offered by universities, high schools, Rotary

International and sister-city organizations. Transitions Abroad (www.transitionsabroad.com) is a great resource for links and information on educational programs.

Language Learning — You may have a desire or need to go to India to learn Hindi or any one of the 18 other major languages spoken. If you are living in the country for an extended period of time, you might consider taking classes so as to better communicate with your neighbors and colleagues.

While language schools dot the country, they are most prevalent in major cities. An Internet search by city and desired language will result in numerous options. These schools offer a wide range of course lengths, from a few hours to months, and are quite affordable. Expect to pay about $6 per hour for formalized lessons through a school.

Alternately, you could employ someone local to provide you with private lessons.

↬ Outdoor Sports

Trekking — India's Himalayas offer superb trekking opportunities without the crowds of Nepal. Outdoor types shouldn't miss the chance to discover this beautiful part of the world.

Garhwal, Ladakh, Himachal Pradesh, Sikkim and Jammu & Kashmir all offer brilliant trekking. It's refreshing to be away from India's crowds in these pristine wilderness areas that offer wildlife encounters and dramatic scenery.

Spring and fall are the best times to visit these regions except Ladakh and Jammu & Kashmir, which are best experienced from June through September. Because the rest of India heads to the hills during the sweltering summer months, this is also the most crowded time.

Easily obtained permits are required for Sikkim, and the political situation in Jammu & Kashmir remains tenuous with sporadic local fighting. It's possible the area may be closed to travelers. Check with the Indian embassy or consulate in your country for up-to-date information.

A reputable travel company can provide you with a guide, cook and porter, making the hard work simply the trek itself. If you're inclined to save your chai money, however, it's quite possible to carry your own pack and trek the more popular routes on your own.

Boating — There's nothing like the splash of water slapping up against your kayak, canoe, raft or face on a hot day on the subcontinent. The fresh air in the Himalayas coupled with blue skies and a serene environment will help you forget the traffic and dust of Delhi in a moment.

If water sports are your thrill, consider riding the rapids in northern India, where a range of river rafting opportunities abound in the mountain areas. Sikkim, Himachal Pradesh, Uttarakhand, Ladakh, Jammu & Kashmir, Leh and northern West Bengal are all good places to find outfitters. Rafting companies are also in larger cities and villages and can make arrangements for day or longer trips.

The major rivers for rafting are the Ganges, Teesta, Beas and Brahmaputra. The best time on the water varies with the region but most months provide an opportunity somewhere in the country. You can also raft in Goa and Maharashtra States.

Trips can be booked either in advance or upon arrival, depending on the season. Not all tour companies are open in the off-season and during the busy season they may be booked up in advance.

While there are opportunities to white-water kayak in the rivers listed above, you might prefer a quieter boating experience by kayaking or canoeing along the coastline, in a lake or in a gentle river. India's seas can be unpredictable, however, so proceed with caution if you prefer the open waters.

Canoe trips are available in Kerala's backwaters, as are short or long stays on mobile houseboats (though you won't be doing the steering in these cases). These backwaters offer a serene experience in this warm-weather southern state.

Diving and Snorkeling — The Andaman Islands, a string of islands located in the middle of the Bay of Bengal, have always been considered India's premier spot for scuba diving and snorkeling. Unfortunately, the tsunami of December 2004 destroyed much of the island in the southern part of the archipelago, where it's believed between 8,000 and 15,000 people were killed. (A sad side note — much of the relief money that poured in reportedly disappeared and has never helped survivors rebuild.)

The Indian government has enticed low-wage government employees to consider the area for vacation in order to help the tourism industry rebound. As a result, locals are now complaining that this influx of budget Indian vacationers is keeping luxury travelers away. You can do your part by visiting the area and supporting local businesses.

Another popular diving and snorkeling area is the islands of Lakshadweep. These are located in the Arabian Sea, off the coast of Kerala. Only three of the islands allow foreign visitors and accommodations are generally government-run facilities with the exception of the Bangaram Island Resort. While the accommodations here are basic, they include beach huts with palm-thatched verandas. Because of its slight currents, this is a great place for beginning divers and those wanting to take lessons.

Both sets of islands are best visited between December and March.

Skiing — Skiing is in its infancy in India and has a short season. As a result, the slopes are generally wide open, but the facilities, lifts, cable cars and rental equipment are not always reliable. Power outages are common, but rental rates and ski passes are cheap.

Some of the best skiing can be found in Gulmarg in Jammu & Kashmir, where skiers compare it to backcountry skiing with a lift. Ungroomed trails lure experts who enjoy the relatively crowd-free experience. Other regions that continue to draw downhill and cross-country skiers as well as snowboarders include Garhwal in Uttarakhand, and Solang Nullah and Narkanda in Himachal Pradesh. Heli-skiing has also entered into the sports fray.

Bicycling — Forget the French countryside. Ship out your Cannondale and hit the always fascinating roads of India. Unless you've got vast amounts of time (and energy!), choose a region, season and terrain that suits your abilities.

You can easily plan your own adventure. You're unlikely to starve, lack for a place to sleep or break down without a dozen "mechanics" ready to help you. With a variety of topography, from twisty mountains to the fields of India's finest spices, you'll have an opportunity to visit with the locals, smell India (at its best and worst) and dive into the richness of its culture and environment. Consider bringing a collapsible bike such as a Bike Friday (www.bikefriday.com) for easier shipping.

If you're more inclined to group travel with a support vehicle and would prefer that someone else handle your arrangements, tour companies specializing in bike adventures can make all necessary arrangements, including the shipping (or renting) of your bike.

↬ Spectator Sports

Cricket — If you are a fan of cricket, there are few countries that make cricket-watching more exciting than India. I was surprised to discover that every boy in every village in every state knows how to play the game. I watched it being played on empty patches of grass located in the middle of a city, on the side of railroad tracks, in the dirt and in garbage dumps, and being broadcast on televisions in bars and restaurants.

The game was brought to the country during the British occupation. Though it is not the official national sport (that's actually field hockey), fervor and excitement for cricket abound, particularly with regards to international matches.

The national teams are overseen by two leagues, the Indian Cricket League (ICL, www.indiancricketleague.in) and the Board of Control for Cricket in India (BCCI, www.bcci.cricket. deepthi.com). For general information, try CricInfo (www. cricinfo.com) or either of the leagues' websites. The international team does not follow a regular schedule of matches, but coverage in newspapers and on television is heavy when they are playing.

To anyone not familiar with the game, it appears complicated and drawn out, with matches being played for days on end and with teams scoring in the hundreds of runs with their wickets and bats and balls.

Regardless of your interest level in cricket, watch the movie *Lagaan* for an excellent introduction to the game and to better appreciate the fanaticism behind their excitement.

Tennis — Tennis is generally played by middle- and upper-class Indians. In recent years, however, a number of young rising stars in India's tennis world have made their mark internationally, boosting the popularity of the game in the subcontinent. Most notably, Sania Mirza gained renown when she became the first Indian to rank in the top 50 of the World Tennis Association and in 2007 was the first Indian woman to be seeded in the U.S. Grand Slam.

True to conservative India's nature with regards to women, her success has also been controversial. She's been accused by Islamists of not wearing proper Islamic clothes on the court (can you imagine her playing in a burka?), and she faced possible prosecution when she was seen resting her bare feet (always considered dirty by Indians) next to an Indian flag during a press conference.

The sport has definitely gained in popularity and, despite what the clerics might believe, these tennis stars have become positive role models to young women (and men) who are looking to further themselves in careers, whether in sports or as business professionals.

3.

CULTURE SHOCK

INDIA can be one of the most rewarding countries in which to travel. It's culturally rich,
openly religious, densely populated and complicated beyond measure. These same attributes
make it one of the most difficult countries in which
to travel. Learning more about the culture, preparing yourself for the challenges, and being open to
its extremes — wealth and poverty, beauty and
unsightliness, kindness and unscrupulousness —
can help you derive the most from your journey.

⌘ Male-Dominated Society

I was dining with my partner, Jon, in Delhi on our last night in India. The restaurant was popular among tourists so our visit was not unusual. After a pleasant meal, we each ordered ice cream for dessert. The waiter returned from the kitchen and told Jon his choice was not available and offered an alternative. He then returned with only Jon's dessert. When I asked for mine, he said that it was also unavailable and insisted that he had told me so earlier. I explained, "No, you told him that his was not available, but you never spoke to me." This sort of interaction was common during my early travels to India, but this was the first time I had experienced such blatant disregard more recently.

Overall, India has become more socially progressive, with women making their way into professional and political positions that were unthinkable just a few years ago. While my experience with the dessert may have been an anomaly in a city like Delhi, the fact remains that women play a diminished role in Indian society, particularly in rural communities.

As a traveler, you'll find it easy to recognize some behavior that will immediately strike you as sexist. Men hold the majority of jobs — they'll be your drivers, waiters, salesclerks, hotel managers and, often, your tour guides. Indian men are more likely to engage in conversation than women and, if you're traveling with a man, he will be spoken to, not you.

I met a couple of Australian gals in Darjeeling who had just arrived from Kolkata, their first stop in India. They had expressed absolute amazement that so few women were seen on the streets. It was the men that dominated every sidewalk. I had become so accustomed to this that it was a surprise for me to hear, but it is so true.

Women are an integral part of the culture but in a more traditional fashion. They are responsible for the home — they cook (when a full-time servant is not employed to do so); take care of the family, including their in-laws; and sometimes work to provide a second income for the family in urban areas.

Though illegal, infanticide and abortion of girl babies is not uncommon. Having a girl is seen as a liability since she will likely contribute little income and will eventually cost the family a dowry (which is also illegal but still a common practice).

After marriage, a woman and her husband are expected to live with his parents, where she becomes both the caretaker and homemaker. If she is doing an unsatisfactory job, she may be killed by the family in what is known as a "bridal death." She may be doused with a flammable liquid and burned in what is reported to authorities as a "kitchen accident." Beatings by the husband, to the point of death or suicide, are also considered bridal deaths.

↫ Touts

A tout is someone who solicits you for your business. An Indian tout is someone who incessantly solicits you for your business, following you through the streets from the moment you leave your hotel, exit the train or get out of a taxi. Given the desperately poor situation of so many Indians, it's understandable, but it's still disturbing, particularly for women travelers, as we may be perceived as more vulnerable and therefore targeted more frequently by criminals.

While in Varanasi, I learned yet another way one can be followed by a tout. Simone and Rahel from Switzerland and I were making our way to the guesthouse where we planned to stay. An Indian man was walking in front of us, making small talk about hotels and renting a boat on the Ganges. We insisted that we didn't want his services and asked him to go away, but he wouldn't heed our requests. When we arrived at the guest-house, he told the manager that he had recommended the hotel to us and insisted on a commission. We furiously denied his involvement, explaining that the referral came from some friends who were already staying there. Who knew you could be followed by someone walking in front of you?

Agra, Varanasi and Jaipur are the cities where I've encountered the most tenacious touts. No matter where you are, however, the consistent bombardment of these salesmen who aggressively pursue you will surely wear you out. Hotel touts "greet" you at the train station to convince you they have the cheapest and best room for rent. Taxi and rickshaw drivers follow you down busy streets until you concede. Shopkeepers accost you on sidewalks, offering rugs, clothes and jewelry. Self-proclaimed experts offer their services at popular tourist sights, insisting that you need a personal guide.

On occasion you may actually need a tout's services. Perhaps you've arrived in a city without a hotel reservation or you need a rickshaw ride across town. Stephanie backpacked solo for a couple of months and learned to embrace what these unyielding gentlemen had to offer: "I loved touts because I could get off the train and have people competing for my business. I took advantage of the fact that they would drop their prices against one another. I also felt safe having their help."

Hot Tip! Use the number of touts vying for your business to your advantage. Don't accept the first offer from a hotel representative or rickshaw driver. Bargain hard for a good price.

If you're not interested in a tout's services, ignore him and continue walking. Denise, who explored much of the country during two months of travel, advises that you "walk around like you own the place. Otherwise, everyone will try to take advantage of you. Make it look like you know where you're going. If you have to ask for directions, do it with confidence. You always have to be on your game." Also, don't make eye contact, and don't feel like you have to be polite.

⌘ Western Curiosity

After exiting the palace in Mysore, I was mobbed by a group of young women wanting my autograph. My first book had just been published and, for a brief moment, I thought word had spread to south India that a travel writer had arrived. I quickly got over that fantasy and realized that these women were interested in my light skin, blue eyes and blond hair.

The women, dressed in beautiful saris and with long braided black hair, swarmed me while they giggled, touched my arm and asked me to sign the palms of their hands, since they lacked paper (and my newly published book).

You don't have to have fair features to be the object of curiosity. Anyone obviously not Indian (including non-resident Indians who dress and hold themselves differently than the locals) may cause quite a stir.

My experience was minor compared to that of Quinnette, a tall, full-figured black woman. She attracted a lot of unwanted attention, and though it was trying at times, she stayed good-natured about it, recognizing that "they stare because no one has ever said it's not OK to stare. One time in Varanasi, we were walking along the ghats where they were floating candles. Every person was staring — every rickshaw driver, every person — and I just had to go back to the hotel as a refuge. When it got to be too much, I would just go inside and remind myself that it was a bad time that you must take with all the good."

Connie is a writer and journalist who lived in India for four years. She also found the attention a little overwhelming at times and she attracted even more stares when she traveled around India by motorcycle for five months. During that time Connie felt the need to retreat and to take care of herself. She found this easy to do, even in the smallest of towns. "After being on the road for eight or nine hours, I would seek out a pedicure and facial, and get some pampering or oil treatment for my hair. It was great because I had all this grime on me all the time and this pampering was a relaxing time for me. You need to be alone at times. If you feel like people are always trying to help or sell you something, it's very tiring. I would sometimes stay someplace and just sleep and not interact until I was ready for it."

You may never shake the feeling of awkwardness that accompanies the staring. The best you can do is smile like a prom queen (but avoid eye contact with men so as to steer clear of any sexual miscues) and be on your way. If you are unable to remove yourself from a situation (if you're on a bus, for example), attempt to align yourself with other women and ignore the person who's staring as best as possible.

Hot Tip! Find a retreat other than your hotel room; try a quiet space such as a temple, school, university library, park or garden. People-watching can rejuvenate you as much as, if not more than, watching a movie or CNN in your room.

At five-foot-nine and blond, Jamie had her own struggles. "I like to be inconspicuous and be by myself. Some days, seriously, I had a breakdown and didn't want to leave the hotel."

These are not unusual feelings and there will be times when you'll need to retreat. Honor your need for this downtime in order to gather your reserves for your next outing. You'll enjoy your journey far more if you do.

Indians will make it their business to introduce themselves and ask you lots of questions about your family, income, marital status and job. In addition to simply being curious, they ask these questions in order to place you in a hierarchy compared to them. You already assume a certain degree of status as a rich tourist, but your answers help to further clarify your standing. No harm is meant and, by Indian standards, these questions are not considered too personal. You may certainly engage in conversation if it feels right, but as a woman it's generally best for you to not quiz a man back, as he may think you are taking an interest in him.

↣ Oh the Humanity!

Though India covers only about 2.5 percent of the world's landmass, its population exceeds more than 15 percent of the planet's population with more 1.2 billion people.

Cities are bursting at the seams as villagers move there to find work. Unemployment is high and low-income housing projects (slums) abound.

Because of the crowds, travel to India can be exhausting! As a traveler, you'll be forced to fight your way to the head of lines and through packed trains, metro cars and bus stations, and you'll learn to elbow your way through markets and tourist sights.

You may find that popular routes on public transportation sell out quickly — leaving you stuck overnight in a dusty village you hadn't planned on visiting for more than a few hours when you find all the trains are booked.

And you'll quickly discover that you have very little alone time. A café that you had hoped to use as a base for writing will be filled with Indians, loudly socializing, gossiping and perhaps even speaking with you.

↩ Caste

Though it may not be obvious to foreigners' eyes, the caste system is still alive and well in India despite anti-caste laws.

Based on a social hierarchy, this system is defined by literally thousands of subtle classes based on a person's heritage. Professions, marriages, social status and living conditions are all influenced by the caste system, which is more strictly adhered to in rural communities than in cities.

Hot Tip! Be a good traveler and show respect to all people, from the person who sweeps the rubbish off the train floor to the monk at the Buddhist temple.

↩ Guests Are Gods

During my first trip to India, I was a cheap backpacker. Accommodations consisted of $2-a-night cement-block rooms with little ventilation and loud noise reverberating throughout the guesthouse. Toilets were squat. Bed bugs were abundant. Mosquito nets were lacking. I was in culture shock and my interaction with the locals didn't go much farther than trying to scare away rickshaw drivers vying for my attention and rupees.

After that first trip, I often heard it said that Indians are the most hospitable and generous hosts on the planet. I never could relate to that observation because I hadn't had the opportunity to meet many locals. Seventeen years later during my next journey, I finally understood what others had for so long been telling me. Indians are, quite frankly, the most curious, friendly and helpful hosts I've ever met.

While riding an overnight train from Varanasi to Siliguri, Shivala, an Indian woman sharing my compartment, taught me a phrase: "In India, guests are gods." She explained that simply being in their country makes you a guest — and you are treated accordingly. Once I heard this phrase, I reflected upon the myriad ways in which I had already been the recipient of the generosity of the Indian people — the same generosity that has continued throughout my journeys there.

In order to meet the locals and get a sense of their hospitality, Maliha, who travels there often to visit family, has a great suggestion: "It helps to hang out where the locals are and not be afraid to ask for advice. Be open and receptive. People will always give you advice whether you like it or not. As a foreigner, you stand out, and that's a good thing." Of course, if you're on your own, you'll want to be more cautious about accepting advice or invitations. Men usually have an ulterior motive! Listen to your gut and extract yourself from any potentially dangerous situation immediately.

Hot Tip! When you're the recipient of local hospitality, reciprocate with attention, small acts of kindness and little gifts where appropriate.

3. CULTURE SHOCK

꩜꩜꩜ Laura's Story ꩜꩜꩜

While in Mysore, I had a whirlwind day. It started with a 12-year-old tout/con-artist-guide named Maruti convincing me that the Mysore Palace was closed in preparation for *Diwali*. He then gave me a tour of the city. The day included stops at a fragrance factory, a sandalwood shop, the butchering area at the market to purchase a live chicken, a sunset dinner in a humble Mysore home and a trip to the Mysore police station!

After a full day in the city we ran into Maruti's father, Kunjax, who invited me for dinner. We walked to their neighborhood, where I was widely introduced. I met the schoolteacher, the men sitting on the front step, many aunts and uncles and dozens of children.

I felt like an ambassador, an honored guest and a sideshow spectacle all rolled into one.

Of the 50 or so people I met, only Maruti, Kunjax, and his younger brother, Danesha, spoke English, but everyone was friendly and curious. Adults and children alike giggled at the ritual of shaking hands and saying, "How do you do?" The neighborhood kids loved playing with my stopwatch and camera. I walked away with half a roll of pictures taken by Maruti and the other kids.

This was not a family with servants. Maruti's mother, Prema, made a simple dinner of spicy fish and rice. We all sat together on the floor of their one-room home. The pink painted concrete walls enclosed a small Ganesh shrine, a bedroll and thin woven sitting mats. They had running water in a floor sink in the corner, but no electricity. We ate dinner as the sun set and the streetlights shone through the open door on that warm late-fall evening. Prema demonstrated how to use my fingers to eat the fish by pinching it carefully to check for bones (of which there were many) in the dim light.

It was not, however, a stress-free day. At each stop on Maruti's tour I was pressured to buy things, but I went into the "tour" with my eyes open, expected nothing less and enjoyed myself immensely. Shockingly, on our way to their home, Kunjax was roughly thrown into an iron fence and interrogated by a local policeman. I rode in the back of the police jeep with him and Maruti to the station. Later, Kunjax said that the officer had wanted a bribe since he was obviously with a wealthy foreigner.

Meeting the neighborhood was an incredible experience but as soon as we sat down to dinner, Kunjax kept bringing up the topic of money. How much I had...how little they had...how much X amount of dollars could buy. It was uncomfortable. Finally, at dinner's end, he asked me for $200 to help pay for Danesha's schooling. It was far more than I could afford and the request felt like a violation of the good will of the whole afternoon. On top of that, I didn't trust Kunjax. He was very welcoming, but in a tipsy sort of way, and, of course, I had already seen that he was not exactly considered an upstanding citizen by the police. The evening ended with sincere goodbyes to Maruti and his mother, but I declined the escorted walk back to my hotel in favor of a rickshaw and was greatly relieved that one was readily available to whisk me away.

During my Mysore "tour" I purchased $5 to $10 worth of items from the jacaranda fragrance factory where Maruti's grandmother worked and at his uncle's sandalwood shop. I also contributed a little money for dinner and purchased a young chicken for Maruti as a thank you for his services. Later, I mailed duplicates of my Mysore photos back to Kunjax to share with the neighborhood.

I later learned that the palace had been open that day; I just hadn't walked far enough around to reach the entrance. And, I learned that the week before two other exchange students from my school had been intercepted by Maruti near the palace. While they didn't spend a day with him, they could vouch for his German and Italian language skills as well as his English. Such a talented kid!

Overall, it was fantastic. I never felt so engaged with an Indian community as I did on that day.

๛ Home Sweet Home

Indian homes are generally simple dwellings that don't include a lot of embellishment. Absent is the large number of photos, artwork, knickknacks and other items that Westerners accumulate. Instead, practical items are in plain view, such as dinnerware, the television, computer, books, CDs and a religious shrine. Even middle- to upper-class families have little need to adorn their homes with items that are nothing more than eye candy or status symbols.

Hot Tip! When entering a home, be sure to remove your shoes; they are always considered unclean.

Kitchens are not equipped with all the trappings of a Western kitchen. Expect only a stove top with burners for cooking rice and dahl rather than a full oven. Stoves run on gas from refillable tanks rather than from city pipes.

Many homes now have built-in filtering or purifying systems, making it OK to drink the tap water. Don't be shy about asking your host if the water is filtered. See Chapter 9, Your Health, for more info on staying healthy with regards to the water.

Given Indians' thorough delight in treating their guests well, you may find that your hosts will attempt to feed you to the point of explosion. You may insult them if you don't eat three or four servings at one meal. Pace yourself, assure them that the food is wonderful and be aware of the amount of food you're consuming. I have yet to determine how Indians can eat so much (and expect me to) and not have the obesity problems of North America.

It isn't necessary to give a gift if visiting someone's home, although it is very much appreciated. When staying with a family in Pune, I listened for cues from my hosts, discovering that they liked bird-watching and painting, and purchased books from a local bookstore on those topics. The gifts were very well received. See Chapter 11, Pack It Up, for some other ideas.

Eating with Your Right Hand

There's nothing yummier than wrapping up your rice and dahl in a scrumptious *paratha* and biting into all its goodness after you've soaked it in some *raita*. There's only one catch: Make sure that you're eating it with your right hand only. Your left hand should only be used in place of toilet paper.

Hot Tip! If eating with your right hand seems impossible, visit an Indian restaurant at home and practice before going to India. Your waiter or host will be eager to help you out and, after explaining your travel plans, you're likely to make new friends in the process.

See Chapter 8, Feasting, for more specific information on eating with your right hand.

Because your hands play such an integral part in dining, always wash them prior to eating. In restaurants there is usually a sink located either right outside of the restroom or in some other obvious location. In private homes, you may find a sink near the dining room for this purpose. Otherwise, ask your hosts for the best place to wash up. Alternately, use sanitizing hand wipes or gel to cleanse your hands. The hand wipes are great for cleaning the table and your cutlery when at a restaurant.

Poverty

I was deeply saddened when I arrived in Mumbai via train. I could see garbage piled alongside the railway tracks for miles. Boys played in these mounds of trash, while young and old

3. CULTURE SHOCK

45

alike pissed and shat amongst the rubbish while the train slowly rolled by.

With six million inhabitants, Mumbai has the distinction of being home to the largest slum on earth. While these slum dwellers make up 60 percent of the city's population, they are crammed into just 6 percent of Mumbai's landmass. In addition to the railway slums, shantytowns line the roads, with tin shack after tin shack butting right up against the roadway.

The extreme poverty is a very difficult thing for most Westerners to comprehend. You'll be forced to witness it in the burgeoning slums and in city streets. The homeless set up camp on sidewalks and street medians with cooking stoves, blankets and makeshift tents. Their daily life — eating, washing and sleeping — takes place in public. India doesn't have a welfare system in place to support the destitute. The population is too large and the corruption runs too deep for the government to provide for such services.

Margaret visited India with a tour group and, while she enjoyed her visit, she found herself trying to understand the implications of what she saw. "For me, it's a moral conundrum. How do I make sense of this part of the globe where people are in such need for food, water and housing? Have we lost our shared human perspective? In my life in America, I have everything I need and more. But in India, you've got this population who lives without even the basic necessities. It makes me more conscious not only about my footprint, but what it is that I can do either at home or in India to help those in need."

As a first-time traveler to India, you may find these scenes so disturbing that you want to immediately go home. Unless you do choose to leave, you can't ignore the poor. But you can learn to accept the situation as part of Mother India, empathize with and respect those who are less fortunate and support organizations designed to help these people directly, either through financial giving or volunteering. Refer to Chapter 2, Follow Your Passion, for ways to volunteer.

↝ Beggars and Street Children

Beggars flock to cities where tourists and middle-class Indians are most prevalent. Women with babies and men with deformities, debilitating injuries or amputations roam the streets asking for handouts.

More heart-wrenching to see are the street children. In Delhi, when stopped at a red light, you can't avoid having a child longingly knock on your taxi window or pull on your sleeve (and heartstrings) if you're in a rickshaw. While you're sitting in traffic, the children perform circus-like acts, tumbling somersaults or banging on a drum while dressed in tattered costumes and makeup.

These children are, more often than not, performing on behalf of the local mafia. They have either been kidnapped from or have been given up by their families in order to pay off a debt. This makes them enslaved to someone who has control over their take — your rupees.

Though I'm deeply affected by these experiences, I resist giving money to these beggars because it potentially perpetuates the cycle.

Jessica spent two months studying yoga and volunteering in Mysore. As a volunteer, she learned what types of things made a difference. "I would make peanut butter sandwiches or carry crackers and give out food, but I would never give money. At the nearby bakery, when a kid would ask me for something, I would just have him point at what he wanted and buy it for him."

To help lessen the shock of the street life you might encounter, Nina, who travels to India yearly, has some sound advice. "Familiarize yourself with the culture by watching movies like *Salaam Bombay*. This will prepare you better than the Bollywood movies that don't show the real India."

↝ Toilets

I first encountered a squat toilet in southern Thailand while I was on my way to India for the first time. It was a hole in the bathroom floor and I could see the river below me. In this same river, children were swimming and adults were brushing their teeth! I was in shock.

During the next three months in India, I got used to the squat toilet, no matter where the sewage landed, and now I don't blink an eye when this is my only option.

You won't find a sign for a "bathroom" or "restroom"; it's simply called "the toilet." In public areas, you'll find that the squat toilet is a ceramic hole built directly into the ground or floor. A foot peg on each side keeps you from slip sliding away. Aim is essential but with a wee bit of practice, you'll do fine.

The contents of your pockets can easily fall out when using a squat toilet, so empty them ahead of time or zip them up. You don't want to have to go fishing for your camera, keys or money.

Jessica learned how to stay clean when using these toilets. "Roll up your pant legs when you go because the floor around the toilet can be really dirty." Indeed.

Budget hotels, trains and public buildings usually have a squat toilet with perhaps (but not always) a Western-style facility as well. Mid- to higher-end hotels almost always have Western-style toilets, as do homes where the family has more connection with the West and more money. Toilets in public buildings such as libraries, schools and museums will often be cleaner than those in restaurants.

Regardless of the toilet style, rarely will toilet paper be available. Instead, you'll find a spigot and water bucket next to the toilet. You use water and your left hand to clean yourself. If this thought offends you, carry your own toilet paper.

Hot Tip! In addition to carrying your own TP, be prepared with a small plastic bag in which to deposit it. Bathrooms don't always have wastebaskets, and because the sewer systems can't handle TP, you won't want to "flush" it. Put it in a baggie to toss later.

∽ Baksheesh

Baksheesh is a general term for the money that exchanges hands as a tip, payment for service or a payoff. Put simply, it greases the wheels so that things get done faster and more efficiently.

For tourists, baksheesh might be the additional amount that many service workers (such as taxi drivers) will ask for, or perhaps demand, once the service is rendered. It might also be the few rupees you pass on to a policeman to get your paperwork processed if your luggage is stolen.

Denise traveled with her friend through India and came to a philosophical understanding of the process. "You win some and you lose some. There were a thousand times when we were nearly scammed in India. We looked at it as a balance. We paid 100 rupees for a rickshaw ride that should have been 30. In that case, the driver won. Can you blame them? We have money and they don't. You have to just get used to it."

On a grander scale, baksheesh is what both propels the country forward and holds it back as politicians, policemen, businessmen and others rely on these additional funds to help support their families. Corruption is rampant in India. It's what gets roads built and mass transit stalled as politicians accept baksheesh from car manufacturers, and it's what keeps the electricity on in some business offices while residential neighborhoods go dark.

See Chapter 5, The Practicalities, for more information on baksheesh and tips.

ᴥ Bathing

Bathrooms in hotels and homes are often a small room with a toilet and showerhead without a tub or shower stall. If there is a tub, a shower curtain is rarely used. Don't be shocked when the water from the shower sprays around the room. Sinks are often placed just outside the bathroom for easy access.

Hot Tip! If there's a hook, hang your clothes and towel behind the door to avoid them being sprayed with shower water. Closing the lid to a Western-style toilet will help cut down on the amount of water that gets splashed on the seat.

In a budget hotel in Udaipur, I was assured prior to checking in that there was hot water in the room. The owner failed to tell me that it was only available very early in the morning (6 a.m.) or very late at night (11 p.m.) when no one else was showering. For this girl it's a hot shower or it's no shower, and after a couple of days I was desperate for hot water. I pled with the owner and soon two buckets were delivered to the room, one with scorching-hot water, the other with cold water. Using a large plastic cup for dipping and pouring the water on my body, I found that these buckets of water made a near-perfect bathing experience. I learned to ask for this at subsequent hotels if my hot water didn't work.

ᴥ Sanitation

The sheer amount of garbage that lines highways, city streets and alleyways in India is staggering. There's nary a garbage can to be found, so it's no wonder the streets are filled with plastic containers, bags and compostable foodstuff. Train passengers toss their cookie wrappers, plastic chai cups and fruit peels out the window. People in cars roll down their windows and chuck their fast-food trash into the street or along the roadside. Pedestrians thoughtlessly toss garbage at their feet.

Jamie spent a hot summer in India and found the amount of garbage quite disturbing. "What always surprised me were the piles of trash, even just around the corner from playgrounds, and that all the rivers were clogged. Most of the trash seemed to be evidence of Westernization like juice boxes, cracker and biscuit boxes. It was a packaged Westernized food system in a country that's not prepared for it."

Shivala, my new friend from the train ride, explained the problem as we watched the sun rise over fields of rice. "Packaged products were introduced to us and have become popular just in the last 20 years. It's a new problem and people aren't yet aware of the effect of their trash on the environment. Things are slowly changing and plastic bags aren't allowed in some villages now."

In a mean twist of events, sacred cows eat the plastic bags from garbage piles. This can literally kill them as the bags get caught in their intestinal system.

See Chapter 12, Responsible Travel, on how to be a part of the solution.

~ Arranged Marriages

Arranged marriages are still very common in both rural and urban areas, though the more contact a family has with the West the more likely a marriage will be a love match rather than an arranged one.

Sigrid was surprised by an encounter she had. "We met a young guy who was really nice. He was easy to laugh and seemed quite Westernized. Yet he was 22 and was waiting for his parents to find a good partner for him."

Arranged marriages are now often made through the Internet via classified ads and matching services. Desirable qualities listed include light skin, a good education, the family's background and the health of both the individual and his or her entire family. My friend's parents turned down an otherwise good match for their daughter because there was a history of diabetes in the potential husband's family.

Perhaps as important as the above qualities is the thumbs up or down from a professional astrologer, who is consulted to determine whether the signs of the potential couple line up and, if so, what would be the best date for marriage.

~ Power Outages

Natural resources are strained in India. As a result, the water-powered electrical system often gets shut down. In Delhi, residential neighborhoods have scheduled outages for much of the day while that power is channeled to businesses. This problem will be compounded by the proliferation of shopping malls, business complexes and condominiums opening in the suburbs.

Budget hotels, neighborhood restaurants and Internet cafés often lose power without notice and without a backup generator. As frustrating as it is, it's unlikely to improve any time soon as development explodes without an appropriate infrastructure.

Hot Tip! Be prepared for outages. Carry a flashlight and, when using the Internet, save your emails and documents often to avoid losing your work.

↭ Holy Cows

Ever hear of a McAloo Tikki Burger? No?! This fried, breaded potato-and-pea burger from McDonald's in India is just one of the menu items meant for the huge population of non-beef eaters.

For Hindus, cows are sacred; you'll be hard-pressed to find a beef burger or steak anywhere in this Hindu-dominated country.

Though they are becoming increasingly rare in the larger cities, cows wander the streets freely, causing accidents on highways and blocking traffic and pedestrians (watch where you step!) throughout the country.

Hindus won't eat beef, but they don't hesitate to make a profit from the animal's hide. Muslims physically do the killing in slaughterhouses and butcher shops, while Hindus own leather-manufacturing facilities where they produce shoes, belts and other accessories.

Hot Tip! Jains worship all living animals. You cannot enter a Jain temple while wearing leather, including belts.

↜ Body Language

Spend any length of time in India and before you know it, you'll be doing it, too. Yes, I'm referring to the ambiguous head bob. This side-to-side tilt of the head could mean either yes or no depending on the situation.

While staying with friends in Delhi, we were leaving the house for the afternoon. I was the last one out and asked if I should shut the door. My friend bobbed his head. Oh no, what was I supposed to do? As I started to pull the door shut, my friend said his son was going into the house. OK, I should leave it open.

If you ask a question in which the response should be no, you're very likely to receive a "yes" instead because an Indian doesn't want to tell you no. Phrasing your questions accordingly is important. "Where is the Taj Hotel?" will get you a more accurate response than, "Is the Taj Hotel this way?"

↜ Language

While there are 18 official languages and more than a thousand dialects, English is widely spoken in India thanks to the British occupation. Misunderstandings happen most often when you're being asked for more money by your taxi driver and he can suddenly no longer understand English!

Despite these occurrences, most service-industry workers catering to tourists will be able to easily communicate with you in English. If you wave down a rickshaw driver who doesn't understand you, it should be easy enough to find another one who does.

The farther away from tourist facilities you are, the more you'll find that the locals only speak Hindi and/or the local language

OTHER GESTURES TO BE AWARE OF

1. In much of the country, you'll be greeted with a delightful gesture: hands together in front of the chest, as in prayer, as the person says, "Namaste," which literally means "I bow to you," but also recognizes the spirit in you both.

2. The North American hand gesture for "come here" (curling your index finger while your hand is in a fist) is considered provocative in India. Instead, turn your hand down and wave your fingers toward your palm to motion someone to you.

3. Never pat someone on the head; it's considered rude.

4. Feet are considered dirty; never allow your feet to touch someone.

5. Don't point with your finger. Instead, gesture with your entire hand or your chin.

6. Handshakes are uncommon except in business settings and in larger cities.

of their state. To further complicate the matter, every couple hundred miles the local language changes.

There are ways around these challenges, however. During a hiking trip on the outskirts of Bangalore, my Indian friends and I met a group of local children who were quite interested in this blond gal headed to the top of the mountain. My friend Bhaswati is fluent in four languages (English, Hindi, Bengali and Kannada), but the children couldn't speak any of these. Rather than communicating verbally, I took digital pictures and shared them. We laughed together despite the language barrier.

Some people don't mind the inability to communicate with the locals. Michelle, who works with women's co-ops throughout the country, finds some peace in not having to be fully involved in her surroundings. "I love being anonymous about travel, being in a bubble with a lot of noise but not understanding any of it."

Hot Tip! Carry a small Hindi phrasebook. When you meet someone who doesn't speak English, this can help cross the communication gap.

↝ Widows

As shocking as it may seem, *Water,* the eloquent film from Deepa Mehta, includes a truthful portrayal of the way many widows are still treated in India. Viewed as a burden and a symbol of bad luck by their family and community, they may be ostracized, required to shave their heads and forbidden to wear jewelry. They wear white (the symbolic color of death), cannot remarry and are dissuaded from attending important events such as weddings.

In rural areas, self-immolation, in which a woman kills herself on her husband's funeral pyre, is not uncommon. Otherwise, she might have a very lonely and isolated existence.

There are an estimated 40 million widows in the country and, while they are not all subject to the rigors of these strict rules, there are organizations to support those who are affected. The Guild of Service (www.guildofserviceni.com), based in Delhi, offers programs dedicated to helping marginalized women and their children.

↝ Karma

Karma is the belief in the cause and effect of your actions. In other words, what goes around comes around, whether in this lifetime or the next.

This subtle but prevalent conviction is what makes the poor believe it is their lot in life to be destitute and the rich believe that their wealth is deserved. It's an unquestioning acceptance that life is in accordance with a cosmic law.

Relaxing into this way of life can be quite liberating. While we Westerners try to control the events in our lives and view many situations as unjust, Indians accept the curveballs that life throws at them and then move on.

❧ Servants

My Indian friends in the U.S. say that the number-one thing they miss from their homeland is having servants. What luxury, you might say! In India, however, you don't have to be rich to have someone help you around the house — most families have servants who care for the children, cook, clean, do laundry, drive or run errands.

In a country with an unemployment rate close to 9 percent, employing servants actually helps the economy. It's expected that if you can afford it (and, because employing servants is relatively inexpensive, most everyone but the lower class can), you will employ servants.

❧ Prostitution

Women, men and children are all heavily involved in the sex trade industry in India.

Children, many from Bangladesh and Nepal, are either abducted from their families or sold into India's prostitution rings in order to pay off a family's debt. Women are also forced to work as indentured sex slaves for the same reason. Some women, after being widowed or abandoned by their family, may see prostitution as their only option for survival.

Though prostitution is officially legal, there are laws that keep it underground and less overt than in other cities and countries where it's also legal. For example, brothels are not legal, making it against the law for more than one prostitute to be in a building at the same time. Public solicitation is banned and the sex act cannot take place less than 200 yards from a public place.

Homosexuality is not publicly recognized or discussed in India. Therefore, male prostitution, uh, doesn't exist. OK, it does exist, but it is outright illegal no matter where it takes place.

Not surprisingly, Mumbai, Kolkata, Delhi and the popular tourist state of Goa are all well-known areas for prostitution.

✤ Cremation

During an early-evening stroll along the banks of the Ganges in Varanasi, I stopped to observe a family as they prepared their loved one for cremation. By the shape of the body, wrapped in a white shroud, it appeared to be a small woman. The funeral pyre was carefully built to accommodate her body while a man sat on his haunches, never leaving her side. Eventually, a *puja* was said and the body was burned.

Cremation releases the soul and allows it to pass to another body for rebirth. This is a common practice among Hindus, Buddhists and Jains in India. (Muslims bury their dead — the Taj Mahal being the shining example of a Muslim tomb.)

Many families travel to holy cities such as Varanasi to provide their dearly departed with one final sacred journey, having them cremated at the edge of the Ganges. Pilgrims come from the far reaches of India to bathe in the (extremely polluted) waters, as it's believed that the river's purifying powers will alleviate a lifetime of sins. Many think that water from this mighty river should be the last thing a person drinks (Perhaps that's because it's so polluted, it'd kill ya anyway.)

Quinnette watched a funeral procession as it wound through the streets of Varanasi. "It was very colorful and so incredibly interesting. We're used to being private and closed and the idea of having a public cremation is over the top, but this was really beautiful."

Please remember that photography is forbidden around the burning ghats and you should not disturb mourning family members.

↷ Astrology

One of my favorite beings in the whole world is Akhand, an astrologer/palm reader whom I met in Udaipur when I was looking for a ride to a local temple. A few of us joined him for a day of discovery of both India and ourselves. During our drive, he generously spent his time asking many questions about our birth days, times and locations and providing insight into our lives and personalities (I'm too serious; Jon has a big heart). I'll forever remember his gentle spirit and ability to understand our small group in such a short period of time.

Since then, Akhand has a website (www.bestpalmreader.com) that he's launched and can provide you with words of wisdom about your life via email when you send him details of your birth and/or a photocopy of your palm. He's also quite an entrepreneur!

I first learned of the importance of astrology in Indian society by reading the classified ads for brides and grooms. Astrological signs are always listed as part of the criteria for an arranged marriage.

Beyond marriages, the importance of consulting an astrologer prior to any important event — the signing of a business contract, the pursuit of an investment opportunity, the purchase of a home or car, or a major journey — cannot be understated.

Trained astrologers advertise their services online, on sandwich boards outside of their shops and on posters in windows. Perhaps you'll discover that you were the wife of a maharaja in a past life…

Hot Tip! Go to India knowing your birth date, time and location. Even laypeople may ask about your birth and that of your parents so that they may better understand your background.

❧ Public Displays of Affection

Public displays of affection between romantic couples are frowned upon; avoid any PDA between you and your beloved. Jon and I were quickly admonished by the "PDA police" at a temple when we held hands and gave each other a simple hug.

Same-sex hand-holding is quite prevalent and accepted, as this is considered to be strictly between friends. (Remember, homosexuality is not recognized.)

MAPPING OUT
THE DETAILS

NOW *that you've determined that India is your destination, considering when and where to go, and for how long, will help ensure that you get the most out of your journey. With proper preparation, your travels can be trouble free. You'll need to know, however, how to best tap into the vast number of resources available for your pre-trip planning.*

⟳ Planning

When to Go — Travel in India can be miserable if you're there during the monsoon season or in the north in the cold winter months. While you might normally plan a trip based strictly upon your work or school schedule, in the case of India, consider consulting a guidebook to determine the best time of year for the region(s) you want to visit.

In general, the ideal months are between November and March. This is the coolest time with the least amount of rainfall.

If you live in a cold climate, you can enjoy a wonderful break from the snow by visiting the south, where temperatures are hot year-round. Tropical monsoons begin in late May and remain for a few months. They'll hit along the Kerala coast and then move northeast. A second, shorter monsoon season then slams Tamil Nadu, Andhra Pradesh and Kerala between October and December.

The country's midsection experiences high temperatures throughout the year and heavy rains in the summer. Winters are cool, with monsoon rains in some areas.

Northern India and the Himalayan region are downright freezing during the winter months. The weather is spectacular in July and August, but then the area is crowded with Indian vacationers seeking respite from the heat that blankets the rest of the country.

The western state of Rajasthan is dominated by desert and has some of the country's hottest temperatures. Summers range from 75 to 110 degrees F and winters are cool, between 45 and 75 degrees F. While much of Rajasthan remains dry, Gujarat, just to the south, experiences some monsoon rains during the summer.

Kaydin, the Rotary exchange student, was in India during the 2006 monsoon season that destroyed many homes in the west. During this time, she stayed with a family in their large house. "At night, I saw the water in the streets. The next morning, I woke up and opened the door to find five feet of water in the garden. The family was eating on the second floor because the first floor had been flooded. We had no water, electricity or proper food." Kaydin adds that there was some good that came of this experience. "I saw the family pull together — it was a good bonding experience for us all."

Because she was in India for a full year, Kaydin couldn't avoid the monsoon season. But you can, and should.

Length of Trip — Depending on where you are coming from, getting to India can take a long time and the flight can be expensive. Even direct flights from North America can easily be 14 hours. Cost varies depending on the time of year, but expect to spend between $1,000 and $1,800 for airfare. Given the expense and distance, plan for at least a few weeks of travel in order to adequately shake off jet lag and be able to explore a region or two.

Many travelers prefer to spend far longer in order to absorb the vibes of a given area for an extended period of time. One to six months is not uncommon, and because once you get to India everything is so cheap, it's less difficult and expensive than you might think.

For longer trips, consider renting out your home or subletting your apartment to help offset the expense of travel.

Where to Go — It's impractical to think that you can see all of India in one visit unless you plan to travel for a year or two. Ideally, you will pick a few key areas of interest and, depending

QUICK GEOGRAPHIC FACTS

- India is comprised of 26 states.
- The country is separated from its neighbors to the north by the Himalayas, and is surrounded by water to the east, west and south.
- The country is bordered by Pakistan in the northwest, China and Nepal in the north and Bhutan, China, Bangladesh and Myanmar in the northeast and east.
- The western state of Rajasthan is dominated by the Thar Desert.
- The Western Ghats separate the southern coast from the Vindya Range and Deccan Plateau.
- Approximately 50 percent of the land is arable, making farming one of the major occupations of Indians.
- India is the world's largest tea producer and the third-largest producer of milk and tobacco.

on your length of stay, determine where it is you want to go and how long you have to stay in each location.

Patience and flexibility are important in travel, and more so in India than probably any other country in the world. Don't go expecting that planes, trains and automobiles will run on time. Build in extra time for your vehicle to break down, sights to be closed unexpectedly and serendipity to take hold as you change your own plans to accommodate a festival or an invitation from a new Indian friend.

While the following are not official demarcations of how one might plan a trip, they will provide you with some guidance for making your plans. As Maliha points out, it doesn't really matter exactly where you are, as long as you are enjoying yourself. "There's the tourists' version of India and then there's the independent travelers' version, which is all about getting to know the locals. One great way to do that is by going to places where you'll see everyday life. Not just events or venues. Go to a bookstore or places where you would go in your own life. That way you don't always feel like you're traveling or moving a lot."

As a woman traveler, you might feel more comfortable in larger cities simply because you can blend in more. Though you will still be stared at and pursued by touts and rickshaw drivers, on the whole, the population will have seen enough other tourists so as to not find you completely strange. The more remote the regions to which you travel, the more of an oddity you will be, causing even more undue attention.

Golden Triangle — This area, which includes Delhi, Agra and Rajasthan, is the most visited part of India. The big draw is the Taj Mahal, which is just a few hours' drive from Delhi. It's then a fairly easy jaunt over to Udaipur and Jaipur in Rajasthan and back around to Delhi, completing the triangle. Venturing farther west will plunk you deep into the desert with opportunities for a camel safari.

You can easily book your own trains, buses, and drivers or a combination of these and travel this route independently. However, there are plenty of companies willing to provide you with a packaged tour of this area.

East — Varanasi and Kolkata are the two most popular destinations from the central to eastern part of the country. Visit the ghats along the Ganges River, where pilgrims come from around the country to pay homage to the sacred waters and to cremate their loved ones.

65

Kolkata's reputation precedes it. I avoided visiting this city on my first trips to India because of its reputation for being so desperately poor. Surprisingly, when I finally visited, I found it to be a vibrant, sophisticated metropolis that I thoroughly enjoyed. Traveling through India with friends, Jennifer visited cities as well as smaller villages. She appreciated all that Kolkata had to offer. "I loved it. I enjoyed being in a big city. It was comforting being near water. I felt grounded there because there was so much to do."

South — Along the west coast from Goa southward, you'll find beaches overrun with international travelers baring it all along the Arabian Sea. Venture beyond the young partygoers and you'll discover many interesting areas including French-influenced Pondicherry on the east coast, the high-tech city of Bangalore and palace-filled Mysore.

Don't miss the state of Kerala, a thin strip that boasts some of the most pristine beaches in the country. It's home to the Hugging Mother, Amma, as well as many Ayurvedic centers, ashrams and meditation and yoga facilities.

Middle — From Kolkata to Mumbai, this region is comprised mostly of the western plains and is inhabited to a large degree by India's tribal groups. It sees relatively few tourists, which means that the facilities will be limited but the experiences rich.

Anyone who has been to Hampi will insist this is their favorite place in the whole country because of the unique rock formations, ancient architecture and laid-back feel. In addition, the state of Madhya Pradesh is home to Bhopal, a thriving state capital despite its renown for being the location of the 1984 Union Carbide disaster (in which thousands died when a toxic gas was accidentally released), as well as national parks offering tiger sightings and craftwork from the tribal communities.

Northwest Himalayas — There are two main reasons people travel to the far north: to visit Dharamsala, the home of the exiled Dalai Lama; and to trek in the Himalayas.

April through June and September and October are the best times to visit Dharamsala. These months are between the winter snowfall and summer rains.

Most trekkers head to the hills in the summer when the rest of India is hot, hot, hot. While the political situation in Jammu & Kashmir has been violent over the years, this seems to be stabilizing and the area has been attracting tourists once again. Check with the Indian embassy or consulate in your country for up-to-date information prior to arrival.

Northeast — Some areas of the northeast, including Sikkim, require special permits prior to visiting, in some cases due to political unrest. Darjeeling doesn't require a permit but is no longer the quiet hill station it once was. Billboards now line the twisty road to this "village" and SUVs ply the route carrying locals to markets and travelers to and from the nearest train station in Siliguri.

The tea-growing region of Assam and states farther east are Buddhist-influenced and, despite the threat of revolutionary violence, remain beautifully untouched. Give yourself plenty of time to get around.

Where to Book — It's never been easy to find deals on international flights between continents. I start my search on popular booking engines such as Orbitz (www.orbitz.com) or Expedia (www.expedia.com) to determine what airline has the best fare. I then compare this to the airline's website and book directly if the price is similar. Booking direct (or through a travel agent) means you can tap into customer service if there's an issue with your flight(s).

4. MAPPING OUT DETAILS

Booking engines are valuable for packages that include hotels and/or car rentals. They are also able to combine routes from various airlines, perhaps ultimately providing a cheaper fare. These booking engines do add service fees to the bottom line, however.

For packaged tours, look for recommendations on the Incredible India site run by the Ministry of Tourism (www. incredibleindia.org). The number of companies offering tours is exhaustive, but you can do your own search as well as ask for personal referrals through forums (see Forums, Blogs and Social Networking Groups later in this chapter).

Budgeting — While in Varkala, I treated myself to a nice dinner at one of the restaurants perched along the cliff. Freshly caught seafood was on display and cooked to order at every restaurant. I enjoyed a large serving of prawns, mashed potatoes, roti and fruit juice for under $10. And this was the most expensive meal I had during a month's stay in the country.

India is one of the cheapest destinations you'll ever visit considering the standard of food, level of service and quality of public transportation that's available. Other developing countries are cheap, but not like India.

So, how do you budget for a trip that can be as budget as budget gets, but you don't always want to be on a budget?

Begin by reading through the most current guidebooks. Add at least 10 to 20 percent to prices; they inflate as soon as a hotel or restaurant gets that all-important guidebook listing. Also, guidebooks are published many months (if not a year) after the actual research has been done and do not factor in inflation when quoting prices.

Then, create a budget based on your finances and number of travel days. Transportation, including domestic flights, trains and taxis, will be your greatest unknown expense until you actually get in-country.

Breakfast can be as cheap as a couple of dollars, lunch a couple dollars more and dinner not much more than that. Allow yourself a splurge now and then — it still won't set you back very much. What will quickly add up, however, is alcohol. If you're a drinker, this could very well be the most expensive item you consume.

Other items to factor in are souvenirs and clothes. See Chapter 5, The Practicalities, for more information on traveling On the Cheap in India.

ᕃ Resources

Guidebooks — I'm partial to the Lonely Planet guides because of their breadth of information that spans history, climate, culture and, in the case of India, sample itineraries for this huge country. Though these guides are still bibles for backpackers, they've expanded over the years to include not only budget options but mid- and high-priced restaurants, accommodations and services.

Andrea traveled with a friend for a couple of months and found it difficult to plan out the trip because India is so big, but she found guidebook maps helpful. "I didn't like to use the Lonely Planet guide for food but I found it good for mapping out our route."

Rough Guides also cater to independent travelers but tend to attract the less budget-conscious. They include lots of local color and cultural details. I have found some really unique restaurant listings in the Rough Guides.

4. MAPPING OUT DETAILS

Though I don't carry it with me due to its weight, I always pick up a copy of the Eyewitness Guide for my destination. These are packed with photos and give me inspiration with regards to where I might like to visit and photograph.

Bottom line is that there are lots of guidebook options out there and you should find a series that suits your style and needs. There are a number of independent travel bookstores in North America with a large selection of books and knowledgeable staff to help with your search.

Dining Guides — So much of your India experience will revolve around food. The cuisine is complicated and unfamiliar to many people, therefore you might benefit from picking up a guide dedicated to the country's culinary smorgasbord.

Eat Smart in India from Ginkgo Press (www.ginkgopress.com) includes lots of details (and recipes!) to make eating in India manageable.

Maps — I had suggested to my friends that I would find my own taxi to their home when I arrived at the Bangalore airport from the U.S., but they insisted that they would have a driver pick me up. As there are no street signs near their home, they had to give him step-by-step instructions by cell phone.

This was how I learned that many Indian roads are not even marked with street signage, let alone are they documented on a map. This makes it difficult when trying to find your way around a city or state.

Even so, I love to open up a big map of the country I'm visiting and trace the route that I plan to take. It helps me put everything into perspective, understand the distance I'll be covering and determine if my best-laid plans are even possible.

Hot Tip! Purchase a map of India before arriving, as it's difficult to find a good one in-country.

Online Research — Online research can be a fun process, but it's sometimes difficult to wade through all the muck. Start with a good, trusted portal that aggregates India information for you.

The government-run Incredible India website is a great start. India Mike (www.indiamike.com) is another excellent resource that includes travel and practical articles as well as a forum in which travelers, expats and Indians share information.

Once you have done initial research on the country and region(s) you'll be visiting, you may have more specific questions, which you can simply enter into a search engine. There's virtually no information that can't be found online.

Forums, Blogs and Social Networking Groups — When I began researching travel online, I was put off by the fact that my searches rarely returned what I felt to be credible results. Where were the articles written by trusted travel writers? Instead, I was finding posts from random bloggers talking about their personal experiences.

But what I soon learned after wading through information from these numerous blogs was that there was still a lot of truth in what the masses were writing. I do take this information with a grain of salt, but getting restaurant and hotel recommendations, as well as leads for reliable drivers, has never been easier.

In online forums, you can search for answers and post questions about a specific topic. On sites such as Lonely Planet's Thorn Tree (www.lonelyplanet.com/thorntree), Fodor's Travel

Talk (www.fodors.com/forums) or the India Mike forum, you can sometimes get answers to your questions literally within minutes. These more-popular forums are monitored by people who live in-country and are able to provide up-to-the-minute details about what's happening locally.

On social networking sites such as Facebook (www.facebook.com) and Google Groups (http://groups.google.com), you can find people with common interests and share information.

THE PRACTICALITIES

THERE *may be nothing "practical" about traveling through India. However, understanding the processes, red tape and hoops that you must go through will help create a smooth(er) journey. Let's explore how to make your travels easier.*

❧ Documents

Passports — You must have a valid passport in order to enter India. If you are a U.S. citizen applying for a passport for the first time, go in person to one of 7,000 locations across the U.S. listed on the U.S. Department of State website (www.iafdb. travel.state.gov) and expect a six-week turnaround. Passports are valid for ten years. Canadians can apply at a local passport office listed on the Passport Canada website (www.ppt. gc.ca) for one that is valid for five years. If you are a citizen of a country outside North America, check with your home country's guidelines. You'll need two photographs of yourself, proof of citizenship and a government-issued ID such as a driver's license.

If you need to renew your passport, U.S. citizens can do so via mail by sending form DS-82 along with your most recent passport, two passport photos and funds to cover the fee, to the National Passport Center. All info is listed on the Department of State website. Canadian passports are not renewable, but you can apply for a new one using an online application or you can mail in form PPTC 004, which is downloadable from the Passport Canada site.

Passport processing can be expedited for an additional fee and extra shipping charges.

Hot Tip! Rather than providing your original passport when requested by your hotel, a travel agent or even the police, give them a copy. They will understand if you explain that your passport is at an embassy awaiting a visa stamp (whether it is or not).

Your passport is the most valuable item you'll carry with you when you travel. Keep copies of the front page both at home and in your luggage. Hotels in India require your passport information at check-in, but you should never leave your passport with the hotel desk clerk.

If you lose your passport while traveling abroad, immediately contact the local authorities and the nearest embassy or consulate for your country. Having a copy of your passport handy will make the replacement process a relative breeze. If your valid passport is lost or stolen while you are at home, alert your passport agency and apply for a new one.

Visas — You must apply for a visa prior to your arrival in India. In order to apply, your passport must be valid for at least six months prior to your application date and must have at least two blank pages.

For U.S. and Canadian citizens, the process is pretty simple. India has "outsourced" (their word, not mine) their visa processing to a third party, Travisa Outsourcing (www.indian-visa.com), and the cost is anywhere from $40 to $150 depending on your length of stay, number of entries and type of visa. There's also a $13 processing fee tacked onto this cost. Canadian citizens pay between C$62 and C$200 and must mail their application and payment directly to their nearest embassy or consulate with a prepaid return envelope.

Special Visitor Permits — Some regions in India require special permits to visit. This includes Sikkim, certain areas of Ladakh, some states in the far northeast, the far west Thar Desert, areas near the Pakistani border, and the islands of Andaman and Lakshadweep. Due to civil unrest in some of these areas, it's always best to check with the Indian embassy or consulate to determine how safe a region is at any given time.

Depending on where you go, the permit may be issued upon arrival to the area or you may be required to apply in advance with an official agent. A guidebook can provide specific information on exactly where to obtain permits.

∾ Money Matters

How to Carry Your Money — India is one country where you'll want to pay extra attention to how you carry and handle your money. Opportunistic thieves and crowds abound. As a woman, you will garner much attention and may be seen as an easy target.

In general, I keep larger quantities of cash in a neck pouch or leg pouch (though leg pouches can get bulky). I include my passport (or a copy of it if I have a safe place to store the original in my hotel) as well as any other important documents such as travelers checks.

I then carry smaller amounts of cash in a change purse in my pocket or day bag. This makes it easy for me to pay for inexpensive items such as a rickshaw ride or meal.

Power outages are frequent. Always carry at least some cash as you may find yourself without access to an ATM or credit card machine.

Hot Tip! Carry small bills and pocket change. If you need to pay a taxi driver or other service employee, he will often claim to not have change so you'll end up "tipping" him, perhaps against your will.

If I can put my own padlock on a hotel room door, I often will leave cash and my passport in my room, but even then I lock my valuables in my luggage or in a safe in the room if one is provided. Don't be tempted to leave valuables at your hotel's front desk; some hotel staff are not beyond snatching an item or two. See Chapter 10, Safety First, for more details about keeping your personal belongings safe.

Rupees — The rupee is India's currency. One rupee equals 100 paise, available in 5, 10, 20, 25 and 50 paise coins. Most of the currency you'll deal with, however, will be in the form of paper notes in denominations of 5, 10, 20, 50, 100, 500 and 1,000 rupees.

When you do receive change from a merchant, make sure that the bank notes are in good condition. Many shop owners won't take ripped notes and even beggars don't want them.

You cannot leave the country with your rupees in-hand. You must, therefore, spend them prior to your departure or change them back at the (less-than-helpful) money-changing kiosks at the airport. You'll also need to show a receipt that you changed the rupees at a bank or official exchange kiosk in order to convert them back to your preferred denomination.

Hot Tip! Use up the remainder of your rupees on final purchases including a last meal, taxi ride to the airport, drinks and souvenirs, and change what few rupees you have left at the airport.

As a point of fact, one lakh equals 100,000 rupees; and one crore equals 10 million rupees. You'll see references to these amounts in newspapers, though you will probably never have to shell out this much unless you're considering a home purchase.

On the Cheap — India is one of the cheapest places on earth to travel. Stephanie was there during the off-season (i.e., monsoon-time) in northern India. "I spent $400 over two months and that included transportation, food and hotels." She couch-surfed (see Chapter 7, Lodging Options, to find out about couchsurfing) much of the time or stayed at budget hotels for about $1 per night. Though the rains can "dampen" your plans, this less touristy time certainly has its advantages!

While staying at a guesthouse in a Tibetan refugee village in Delhi, my breakfasts consisted of a large bowl of porridge with bananas, baked Tibetan bread (similar to an English muffin) and two cups of coffee. All this for just two bucks. Even at one of the most expensive dining spots in Jaipur, the revolving restaurant at the Om Hotel, a full-course dinner that included live music cost less than $7 a person. (Note: the restaurant itself does not serve alcohol, but there's a bar located on a different floor.)

Tipping — Tipping in India is not as regular a practice in the service industry as it is in many other parts of the world. Waiters at cheaper restaurants and taxi drivers, for example, won't expect a gratuity (though taxi drivers will surely build in their own "tip" nearly every time), but it's certainly appreciated. A 10-rupee note, for instance, will show your porter or tout that you were happy to have him help you with your bags.

Mid-to-high-end restaurants may add an additional service fee to the bill, which covers what you might normally leave as a tip.

Baksheesh — Though there's a fine line between tipping and baksheesh, the latter is often used as a way to get someone's attention rather than as a bonus for a job well done. It can also include the rupees you hand over to a beggar or the bribe you subtly pay to the policeman to let you pass through a side street on a motorbike.

I've never officially paid out baksheesh to anyone in India. I say "officially" because I know I've been ripped off at times, providing an unintended "tip" to store clerks and rickshaw drivers who got the best of me.

I don't recommend bribing someone of authority, per se, but offering rupees to help a cause or as a fee to help get paperwork processed may give you quicker results.

Bargaining — Bargaining is a very personal matter. No matter your finances, you are rich compared to the vast majority of Indians. Your day bag alone is probably worth more than what most people there make in a month. As a result, there's a delicate balance between not wanting to be taken advantage of and bargaining over what could amount to pennies to you.

Don't begin a bargaining session unless you are really interested in the item. There will be a sense of ill will if you bargain down to a fair price only to walk away from the vendor or shopkeeper.

If you're requesting the services of a taxi driver, massage therapist, guide, etc., settle on a price in advance and write it down so that both parties are in agreement. Insist on sticking to that price unless there was a change in plans, such as requesting your driver to make additional stops or to drive farther than originally planned. I've had drivers try to charge me more because the air-conditioner was turned on or, so one insisted, we drove more kilometers than he originally anticipated.

Many shops will have fixed prices, though there may be some leeway in bargaining if you're purchasing more than one item. In this case, you may be provided one price for your entire purchase, rather than for individual items.

As a foreigner, expect to be charged more than a local for every item you purchase. In a shop in Delhi, I listened in as an

Indian woman bargained on behalf of her American friend. After much haggling, the foreigner gave in to a price only to have her friend continue the bargaining — knowing full well that they were being charged the tourist price.

Hopefully this all sounds like fun. Nina loves the process of negotiating over her purchases. "I always bargain. The first price given is at least three times what it should be. If someone asks 10, I offer one and then we work back up from there." She notes that for more expensive items, "there may be tea involved because it can take time." For her, it's also about connecting with the shopkeeper. "If someone I like is selling an item that I really want and I can afford it, I'll buy it. I know that they'll take that money and be able to have a meal with it and feed their family."

Hot Tip! When negotiating, always write down the price to ensure that what you and your seller are both saying is being understood. The numbers 15 and 50 can sound a lot alike.

Cash — The spiraling U.S. dollar ain't what it used to be and some entrance fees and purchases can no longer be made in this currency. The Taj Mahal, for example, has been known to deny entrance fees paid in U.S. dollars. Euros or pounds sterling are a good backup and all can simply be exchanged at official money-changing kiosks, banks or directly with a merchant.

At all times, I keep enough U.S. dollars and/or rupees to last me a few days in case something goes sideways and I can't access my travelers checks or debit or credit cards. Many businesses are cash based and it may be difficult, particularly for smaller purchases, to find a vendor, restaurant or hotel that will accept a credit card or travelers check.

Credit and Debit Cards — I generally use my mileage-building credit card for larger purchases such as a splurge at a nice hotel or an expensive souvenir. With the exception of Capital One, credit card companies tack on up to a few percentage points as an international conversion fee on all purchases.

Avoid using your credit card for cash advances as the bank could charge as much as 25 percent interest.

Use your debit card at the many ATMs found in major cities and in some smaller villages. If one machine doesn't take your card, try another. In the village of Varkala, I found that the ATMs were quite fickle. On some days my debit card worked at one bank, while on other days it only worked at a different bank.

Travelers Checks — When I first traveled to India, the only way to get rupees was to stand in a long line at the bank and wait for hours while the tellers shuffled you from one window to the next. Ultimately, you'd find one gentleman who would fill out an enormous ledger with your hotel name, length of stay, your next destination, country of origin, passport number, birth date and the name of your first born (joking). Cups of tea and lemon soda were provided to help make this drawn-out process more bearable.

This could easily take three hours (no joking).

Now, exchanging travelers checks can be done quickly and easily at a bank or exchange kiosk found in any town with tourists.

Though many people think they are no longer useful, I never leave home without travelers checks. They are a great backup when the power goes out and you cannot access your credit or debit card and many shops simply cannot accept credit cards.

Keep a register of your check numbers both in your luggage and at home where a friend or family member can access them. I've taken to copying down the numbers in a Word document and emailing it to myself for easy access should I lose them.

American Express and Thomas Cook checks are the best bets. Depending on the strength of each currency, consider getting U.S. dollars, euros or pounds sterling.

Emergency Money — If you find yourself in an emergency situation with no cash, you can have money wired to you via a service like Western Union (www.westernunion.com). It won't be cheap, but if you are in a bind this is one way a friend or family member can help you out.

Black-Market Money — There are indeed times when a bank cannot give you the best exchange rate for your dollars depending on fluctuations in the market and demand for a foreign currency. These situations rarely occur in India and, to stay safe, you're better off sticking with a bank, official exchange kiosk or shop merchant to change money.

If anyone on the street offers you a better rate than the bank (often called black-market money), it is a scam. Though the offer may seem lucrative, you will either be given a stack of worthless bills or shortchanged for your foreign cash.

✎ Languages

English is taught in the schools and is used frequently, though peppered with Hindi, by anyone with an education. You can thank the British for the introduction of English. You'll find that Indians speak a flowery, yet at times stiff and formal, form of English with interesting colloquialisms. Read any local newspaper to get a sense of this.

Quinnette discovered that sometimes words aren't needed to make a connection. "If you say *'namaste'* and bring your hands together in prayer and bow — there's something so humbling and spiritual about that." You, too, will discover many ways such as this to get around language barriers.

↬ Communication

Internet, Email and Blogging — Even rural India is now connected with the outside world via the Internet Though the connection may be slow and unreliable, and the power outages frequent, most remote villages with tourist facilities have at least one Internet café.

I recommend using email sparingly. It's too easy to get caught up in work or family issues when you're tempted to check and send messages regularly. Instead, try blogging.

Blogging is an excellent way to document your journey while keeping in touch with family and friends back home. Set up your own (free) blog on a website such as Blogger (www.blogger.com) and, rather than sending bulk emails, your fans can check out your blog at their convenience. Cary traveled for 14 months in Asia, including India, and had no problems staying connected with home. "I used Wordpress for my blog. I blogged when I was inspired and when there was an available Internet café."

Pam is a travel blogger and regularly updates her travel blog (www.nerdseyeview.com) while on the road. "I used to write letters, but now I blog and have my family and friends check in online. My mom gets email alerts now each time I post!"

Hourly rates at Internet cafés vary, as does the connectivity speed, but expect to pay about a dollar per hour. Avoid entering your credit card number or any other personal information (passport number, Social Security number, etc.) on a publicly accessed computer. Spyware, accidentally or purposefully downloaded onto a computer, can allow others to track your keystrokes, potentially capturing your passwords and credit card information.

Hot Tip! Clear the cookies, cache and history of the Internet browser before logging off so that your personal information cannot be accessed by the next user. If you're unsure how to do this, ask an employee at the Internet café.

Skype — I first used Skype (www.skype.com) while I was traveling solo in India. I was a bit homesick and lonely for Jon, who was back at home. I popped into an Internet café in which the computers were equipped with Skype. I simply logged on and, voila, I was connected with Jon via a web camera.

I was self-conscious about having a full-on conversation with him since there were others in the café, but Skype allowed us to instant message and see each other at the same time. I was even able to move the portable camera around enough to show him street scenes in Kolkata.

Skype is a voice-over-Internet service that you sign up for and then access via any computer with the Skype software installed. As long as the person you're speaking with also has an account, it's free. You can also pay to call regular landlines and cell phones via Skype. With a microphone and headset combination, you can communicate with others across the world and, if there's a webcam connected to the computer, you can actually see each other as well.

Cell Phones — During a trip to India in 2007, I was sure that I was the only person in the country without a cell phone.

Airtel, the dominant local cell phone service, has shops every-where. Even the rickshaw drivers make plans for their next fare via cell phone.

On my next trip, I did carry my cell phone with me and found it to be an inexpensive way to connect with home. Check with your provider — many cell phones now are GSM- (global sys-tem for mobile communications) enabled, allowing you to connect to an international network.

In my case with AT&T, I could place a call directly to the U.S. from my phone and be charged approximately $2 per minute. Incoming text messages were free while outgoing messages cost about 15 cents each. By adding a local SIM (subscriber identity module) card to my phone, calls cost just pennies within the state where I was traveling and about 20 cents per minute to call the U.S.

Unfortunately, each state in India works on its own network. This means that to avoid roaming charges, you need to swap out your SIM card each time you arrive in a new state. If you're moving among states quickly and not using a lot of minutes, this can be time consuming and expensive. You must pro-vide a passport-like photo and fill out paperwork in order to purchase a SIM card. You're then charged an activation fee of about $10 to $15 that includes a set number of minutes.

Public Telephones — Few homes have landlines. If a family doesn't have a cell phone, they head out into the streets to use a public phone. Look for the STD (standard trunk dialing) signs along any street. You might find yourself using an actual phone booth or dialing from a phone that is sitting on a table in the middle of the sidewalk.

Rather than inserting coins, a clock will track your minutes and you'll pay the phone man directly. It's possible to make international, domestic and collect calls from these booths. The going rate to call North America varies slightly, but expect to pay about 14 cents per minute. To place an international call, you must first dial 00 and then the country code for the country that you are calling.

Postal and Delivery Services — The Indian postal service isn't always reliable. While packages and letters may never make it to their destination, postcards do tend to arrive safely. Once you purchase stamps, you may have to use glue (supplied by the post office) in order for them to stick. Ask a postal clerk to frank them with the date so that thieves can't steal the stamps for resale (yes, it does happen).

If you are shipping a package home, it may arrive with no problems at all, but it's also possible your box may never arrive or you may find items missing once it does arrive. Though shipping a package from home is a simple process, it's quite complicated in India.

This didn't deter Laura from sending a 40-pound package home. In the process, she learned how generous Indians are with their time. "You have to have the right mindset. You know that mailing a package won't be the 20 minutes it takes at home — it's going to be four hours. The box I had needed to be wrapped in a sack. I got carted around on the back of a motorbike by someone who helped me get the package wrapped properly. I found over and over that people bent over backwards to help out and they never expected to get anything in return."

If you'll be in India for an extended period of time, you can have letters or packages sent to you general delivery (poste restante), though this service is also unreliable. The sender mails something to you at the post office address and includes your surname prominently displayed in large letters. In theory, you should be able to then retrieve it with no problems. Having items sent to larger post offices is more reliable than to smaller ones and there may be a cost per item to get your mail.

Registered services such as DHL and FedEx deliver to and ship from India. These are far more reliable because you can actually track your package, but they are also quite expensive.

✦ Business Hours

Business hours are generally from 9:30 a.m. to 5:30 p.m. Monday through Friday, with government offices open from 9 a.m. to 5 p.m. Monday through Saturday. Retail shops may stay open later depending on the area and banks tend to have slightly shorter hours. Many offices and shops close between 1 and 2 p.m. for lunch.

✦ Time Zones

The whole of India is in one time zone. Indian Standard Time is 5.5 hours ahead of Greenwich Mean Time. In more practical terms, this is 12.5 hours ahead of Pacific Standard Time (PST) and 9.5 hours ahead of Eastern Standard Time (EST). The half hour is meant to provide more daylight hours across the huge subcontinent.

✦ Festivals and Religious Holidays

Religious and government holidays and harvest festivals may shut down businesses, banks and retail shops. Check local calendars and call offices for detailed information. India's three national holidays are:

January 26 — Republic Day

August 15 — Independence Day

October 2 — Gandhi's Birthday

Other holidays include:

> May 1 — Labor Day
>
> December 25 — Christmas Day

See Chapter 2, Follow Your Passion, for more information on festivals.

❧ Shopping

While in Jaipur, I was having a difficult time finding the silver bangle bracelets that I desperately wanted. Even having found "bangle alley," I could only find ones made of cheap wood or plastic and fake gems. One vendor, however, understood what I was looking for and brought me to a silver shop. $120 and 15 items later, I had what I wanted. I know I was overcharged, but I was happy with the bargains I struck and thankful to have been led to a silver shop I wouldn't have found on my own.

Indian society is based on networking and relationships. Your rickshaw or taxi driver will inevitably want to bring you to his "uncle's" or "brother's" shop for your purchases. The driver will get a commission and you will pay more as a result. As with my bangle purchases, I've had luck with someone bringing me to a shop that sells items I couldn't find elsewhere but, more often than not, I was taken to large overpriced shops where the fixed prices were easily double what small shops that allowed for some bargaining were charging.

Hot Tip! When possible, purchase from small independently owned shops or those that support cooperatives that help provide income for individual tailors and artisans.

Clothing — Buying new clothes in India can be an adventure. Whether you're shopping at a small market stall or a depart-

๑๑๑ Michelle's Story ๑๑๑

I work with a women's cooperative and fair trade businesses in India making handicrafts like bamboo baskets, wooden toys and textiles. It takes a lot for these women to get their businesses started because they have to stand up to the men. These co-ops are often in small villages and the men are very threatened by the women's independence. In one village, the weaving building was burned down by the men three times.

These women are truly artisans but I have access to a market through Playfair Trading (www.playfairtrading.com) that they don't have access to. I can coach them and assist them, but I can't promise that they'll be successful. They have to own that. I can let them know what's popular in the Western market, but they have to do the work. What I do is not charity nor do they want it to be.

People are becoming conscious consumers. Now people are interested in where their products are coming from and they are willing to pay more, but they aren't going to compromise their standards. People will buy the fair trade product if it's fair trade but only if it's quality. I spend a lot of time working with these women on that to let them know who they are selling to. I want them to know who's wearing this and what stores they are selling into.

I get a very positive experience out of India because I see people who are rising up against stereotypes.

ment store, you can get free alterations done almost immediately and items can be so cheap that you'll be hard pressed to stop yourself from buying too much.

For a truly Indian souvenir, take home a sari. Made from either cotton or silk, these are generally worn for special occasions by younger women and more regularly by middle-aged women and the older generation. Many stores specialize in saris, with literally hundreds of fabrics from which to choose. Plan on spending an afternoon poring over your options. There's a reason they serve tea or lemon soda in these shops — it could take hours to choose a pattern!

FabIndia is a delightful store with locations in most major cities. Trendy styles that appeal to Western tastes are created using traditional Indian patterns and fabrics. Half of my wardrobe is from FabIndia!

If you can't find what you're looking for at FabIndia, you can purchase fabrics and have a tailor custom-make an item. I have found that choosing cloth and then having a skilled seamstress create a clone of something else I own works well.

Textiles — Textiles are truly a part of India's, uh, fabric. Gandhi had wanted Indians to burn their foreign-made clothes and support villagers by wearing khadi (hand-spun cloth). Khadi shops that now include handcrafted products of all sorts are located throughout India and the message remains the same; handmade textiles support the locals and provide Indians with a national dress.

Because it is a major industry, textiles are relatively inexpensive. Handwoven silk and cotton, wall hangings, scarves, embroidery and more can all be found throughout the country.

Jewelry — Gold jewelry is worn by Indian women throughout the country with the exception of Rajasthan, where silver is the metal of choice. These are often inlaid with semiprecious stones such as amber, amethyst, rubies, turquoise, coral and more.

Know your stones if you plan to shell out some good rupees for jewelry. Otherwise, you're likely to get taken.

Margaret knew what she was doing and exactly what she was looking for when she made her purchase in Jaipur. "There are a unique variety of gemstones in India. I was looking for a star ruby ring. We went to this one store and it was just incredible for me. It was so much fun because they let me walk outside with a ring on every finger. There I was with a cow standing behind me and a bus passing in front of me with all of these rings on my fingers."

If you're not as knowledgeable as Margaret but you make your purchase knowing (or not caring) that what looks like a ruby or amber may simply be colored glass, then no harm is done as long as you're not paying a lot for it. My earring tree is filled with Indian jewelry and I honestly don't know if they are real silver even though they all carry a ".925" stamp. The most important thing is that I love them and they remind me of India.

Carpets — You can hardly walk down a major city street without being accosted by a shopkeeper ready to serve you up some tea and roll out the carpets for you. Roll up your own sleeves and get ready for some hard bargaining as this may be one of your most expensive purchases. Shop around before you buy as prices will vary. Educate yourself in advance about the various knot counts available in both the cotton and silk varieties and ask lots of questions to ensure you're getting a quality item.

Getting your purchase home is another issue altogether. While the shop owner will probably offer a shipping service, you might consider mailing it yourself using DHL or FedEx. It will be well worth the added expense to ensure your carpet arrives safely.

Handicrafts — The sheer variety of handicrafts available in India is unimaginable. Hole-in-the-wall shops and street vendors selling goods on makeshift tables cover every nook and cranny of a city's sidewalks. Compare prices among shops. Even though items are cheap, be prepared to bargain as prices are rarely fixed in these smaller stores and stalls.

Government-owned handicraft emporiums are an excellent place to start your search for local handicrafts. I used to think of these only as well-stocked but overpriced shops until I started discovering unique gift items there that I literally couldn't find elsewhere. While they are slightly more expensive compared to shops carrying the same items, their variety is unparalleled. Prices are fixed, which makes shopping hassle free.

Handicrafts to look out for throughout the country include sandalwood, incense, jewelry, textiles, carpets, carvings, silk and pashmina scarves, handmade paper and musical instruments.

CDs, Books and Movies — Major cities boast a number of large chain bookstores, including Landmark, Oxford, Crossword, Higginbothams, Odyssey, D.C. Books and Strand Bookstall. In addition, you'll find many small independent bookstores. While the variety of books available is not as wide as in North America, all sell books in English and you can pick up bestsellers, unique Indian-based works of fiction and non-fiction, and books on Ayurvedic medicine, yoga, local birding and other subjects pertinent to India. These bookstores also carry CDs, videos, newspapers and magazines. Prices tend to be cheaper than in North America.

For your listening pleasure, visit an independent music store and pick up the latest Bollywood hits. A CD will set you back no more than a few dollars. I often go into one of these shops humming the tune that's been playing in my taxi in hopes that the friendly staff can help me find this latest hit.

Tea — Tea can be purchased throughout India but you'll have the best luck and variety if you pick up some in the main tea-growing areas of Darjeeling, Assam and Kerala. If you don't want to carry it around, buy it at a shop like Mittal's in Delhi before you leave the country. This small shop is chockablock with tea, offering both bulk and touristy packaged options.

Spices — India is famous for its food and the use of an amazing array of spices. A shopping spree at a grocery or spice store is a must before you depart for home. Prices are cheap and so much of what you'll find will be unique to India. Roopak's, in Delhi, has well-packaged bottles and bags suitable for carrying in luggage.

↝ Media

Newspapers — English-language newspapers are available in cities and at major railway stations. These papers include the *Times of India,* the *Hindu,* the *Statesman,* the *Hindustan Times, Indian Express,* the *Economic Times* and the *Financial Express.*

The front page of most of these papers usually consists of some sensational news (corruption by a much-loved politician, kidnappings of street children sold into slavery or the downward trend of kitchen deaths) as well as the battle for popularity by two of Bollywood's hottest stars (SRK and the Big B). Bollywood gossip receives a lot of coverage as it is more interesting than real-life matters.

Magazines — A number of foreign-based magazines are available at city newsstands and at the airport. These include

93

the *International Herald Tribune, Time, Newsweek* and the *Economist*. *Outlook Traveller* is a magazine published in India that includes excellent ideas for in-country travel as well as beautiful photography.

Television — Satellite television is available in most hotels and all but the poorest of households. Channels include CNN, ESPN, HBO and the Discovery Channel in addition to local news and entertainment programming (including really bad Hindi soap operas).

Radio — Indian radio is much like that in the West. The same songs are played over and over again on commercial stations. The latest popular Bollywood hit gets repeated regularly. This is great if you're trying to catch the name of a given popular song but otherwise quite annoying. It's likely that the only time you'll have access to radio is in a taxi.

◈ Politics

While there are political issues in India that make the headlines, Indians will be more interested in the politics of your home country than they will be in discussing local issues.

Use your best judgment as to whether engaging in political conversation is a safe issue. Political and religious rifts run deep. It's probably best not to broach the subject of Indian politics yourself, as this can be a sensitive topic for many Indians.

Getting Around

THE *mere act of moving between points, whether you're traveling within a city or over a longer distance, will surely be a thrill* no matter *the form of transportation you choose. Decide which mode works best for you based on the amount of time you have to get to your destination as well as your budget.*

∿ Trains

Upon returning to India after 17 years, I was a bit reluctant at first to hop back on a train. Memories of traveling in third class as a backpacker in the late '80s overwhelmed me. I discovered, however, that spending a few more dollars on an upgraded ticket allowed me to have an experience that was (mostly) relaxing, (relatively) comfortable, (pretty darn) safe and (generally) hassle free. It took some getting used to the farting and belching men that shared my compartment, but I have never felt threatened or unsafe on any train ride.

India has one of the most extensive train systems in the world. Trains run throughout the country with the exception of the mountain regions in the north.

The beauty of train travel is that Indians far outnumber tourists (even more so in the less expensive cars), giving you the chance to mingle, observe and get to know the locals. Indians are very curious and interested people — long train rides will surely provide opportunities for thoughtful conversation if you are open to the experience.

Andrea considers train travel to be the highlight of her two months in India. "Everyone would take us under their wing. Someone would inevitably wake us up a half hour before the train arrived at our station, whether we had spoken with them before or not."

Hot Tip! Overnight travel in a sleeper car will help you save on a hotel room, but don't expect the comfort and privacy depicted in the film *The Darjeeling Limited*. Other riders may come and go throughout the night, making for a sometimes noisy experience.

Once you arrive at the railway station, search for your car based on the class type (outlined on page 98) listed on your

ꙮꙮꙮ Simone's Story ꙮꙮꙮ

My boyfriend and I went to India for a week and I had to see the Taj. We took an overnight train that was crazy from Agra to Delhi.

We asked how long it took to get to Delhi and were told two hours. All the touts were trying to get our business for the booking but we did it on our own. We went to the station to find the train to Delhi and, when one arrived, we weren't even sure if it was our train. It was.

Because of the tickets we purchased, we were only allowed in the front car. We then realized we were in this section where the toilets were. It was 104 degrees F. There were chickens. A kid threw up on the train. And there was no air coming through the windows because everyone was blocking them. We couldn't even move. We thought, "Oh no, what have we done?"

Someone came to us and said as tourists we should be in first class. Since it was only supposed to be a couple of hours, we didn't mind. But then it turned into six hours.

The first few hours were really quite fun. My boyfriend had a Rubik's Cube and we were showing the locals how to do it. I had a Sudoku puzzle and we were having competitions with Sudoku and the Rubik's Cube.

The train stopped more than it moved. When we ran out of water, when the toilets were overflowing and when it looked like we were going to miss our plane in Delhi, then it stopped being fun.

We later realized that because we purchased our tickets on the same day, these were the only ones we could get. We should have purchased first-class tickets in advance. We weren't trying to be cheap; we just didn't know.

We arrived in Delhi with little time to spare and had to go right to the airport for our flight. We were totally stinky but happy to have made it in time for our flight.

ticket. There will be more than one car for each class. For reserved seats and sleepers, a sheet of paper listing passengers' names is posted next to the door of the car. You simply find your name to confirm it's the correct car and then start the search for your berth or seat number. It's actually quite organized once you know the process, but there are station masters whom you can ask if you need help.

While the trains aren't exactly known for being on time, given the vast distances they travel, I can forgive their tardiness. On lines with single tracks, the train that is on time always has priority. If your train starts out late, its arrival time will continue to get even later.

The Classes

AC 2-tier — For longer trips, I recommend the AC (air-conditioned) 2-tier sleeper car. In this class, there is an upper and lower bunk (on each side, for a total of four bunks) in each compartment and two additional bunks situated perpendicular to this main compartment separated by a corridor.

Berths numbered 1–4, 7–10, 13–16, etc. provide more privacy as they are located in the compartments, can be closed off with a curtain and are not subject to foot traffic like those bunks on the side, numbered 5–6, 11–12, 17–18, etc.

During the day, the bottom bunk is used as a seat by passengers occupying both the upper and lower tier as well as those riding just for the day. At night, however, you have your assigned bunk all to yourself.

The often dirty and scratched windows are sealed to the outside world. Though it's called an AC car, a fan is what's used to cool things off. These cars are generally quiet since outside food wallahs and beggars are not allowed on. Pillows, sheets and blankets are provided in this class but I'd recommend carrying a sleep sack in case there is any question about the cleanliness of the sheets.

AC 3-tier — These are similar to the AC 2-tier cars except there are three bunks on each side of the compartment rather than two, so there will be six people sharing rather than four. Those assigned to the side bunks may also join you during the day.

Pillows, sheets and blankets are also provided in AC 3-tier.

Sleeper Class — These cars are similar to AC 3-tier in their physical layout but they don't have "air-conditioning" and the windows are not sealed shut. Instead, they have bars on them and the glass windows can be opened and closed. Food wallahs, street performers and cleaners all make their way through these cars. These sleepers tend to be louder with far more activity during the day and night, but it can certainly be more interesting.

The breeze that comes through the windows is generally enough to keep you comfortably cool during the day but can be quite chilly at night if the windows don't shut all the way (and they rarely do). Pillows, sheets and blankets are not provided in this class so be sure to have enough warm clothes and a sleep sack to stave off the cool evenings.

Second Class — For shorter trips, second-class seats may be your most comfortable option as the sleeper cars are only used for longer routes. These cars are often full, with limited seating availability. As a woman, you may feel safer sitting as opposed to standing. This will give you some degree of anonymity and help you feel more protected. Seats are usually hard benches and those meant to accommodate three people will usually be occupied by six as passengers vie for even a hard bench on which to sit.

Musicians, beggars and food wallahs jump on at one station and off at the next, hoping to make a bit of money along the way. I've had some really delightful food that was hot and fresh from these roaming vendors. And, I'll never forget the haunting tune sung by a young blind boy on a train from Delhi to Varanasi. The sound of his voice is still with me nearly two decades later.

Ladies-Only Car — I hopped on a train for a one-hour trip from Kayamkulam to Varkala, Kerala. To my delight, I found myself in the ladies-only car. I was the only Westerner and the object of many stares, but at least I wasn't the only woman! A number of young women made their way over to me as I stood clasping the back of a seat to steady myself. These women shared their food with me as we made small talk during this brief trip.

Michelle, who buys textiles from women's co-ops, enjoys the ladies-only cars. "I find these really interesting because women inevitably will start chatting. Women around the world are the same — we share the same fears and thoughts."

Hot Tip! Look for the waiting rooms at larger train stations that are designated specifically for women. Like the ladies-only cars, these provide a wonderful respite from the staring men.

Eating and Drinking — You'll never starve on an Indian train. In addition to the food stalls at every station, food wallahs hop on and off the cars (with the exception of the more private AC cars) with baskets of fruit and freshly cooked small bites (often tasty and hot) and coolers of drinks. For those in AC cars, you can simply step outside during stops to find these wallahs walking the platform. You may also place an order with the conductor and a hot meal will be delivered to you at mealtime, often for a dollar or less.

On one journey, I had ventured off to the toilet early in the morning. On my way back to my berth, I helped myself to a cup of chai from a large silver container sitting at the entrance to my car. It wasn't until the chai wallah came around selling his hot drinks yelling, "chai chai chai, coffee coffee coffee", that I realized this was his business. Embarrassed, I apologized profusely and paid for my cup, which cost five rupees (about 12 cents).

Where and How to Book — Many train routes sell out quickly, even in the off-season. Sleeper cars are limited and fill up particularly fast. If you're on a tight schedule and want a long-distance train, book at least a week in advance. Otherwise, you risk getting wait-listed, having to buy a second-class ticket or getting stuck in a town you're dying to leave.

The easiest (but costliest) place to book your ticket is through a tour company or at your hotel. They will either have access to train information via the Internet or have a *Trains at a Glance* timetable that lists all the train routes and departures. In this latter case, they will simply place a call to find out ticket availability.

Tickets will then be printed out, if they are booked online, or delivered by a runner who goes to the train station to pick up the actual tickets on your behalf. In either case, the agent and/or runner will charge anywhere from 50 rupees to 200 rupees ($1 to $4.50) for their service.

Hot Tip! Always ask how much the service fee is up-front. If you don't, you're sure to be charged whatever the agent feels he or she can get away with.

If you're told that no tickets are available, ask for a tourist-class ticket. These cost a few dollars more and are reserved for foreign tourists. You may not be given this option up-front so be sure to ask the ticketing agent.

The cheapest way to book is to turn up at a train station and buy your ticket directly. You can purchase a ticket for all routes at all stations, so it's possible to book well in advance if you know your schedule. Larger train stations have a foreign tourist office where the agents regularly service foreigners.

When booking through a tour company, you have to be careful to make sure you are getting the ticket you've paid for — check the class of service indicated on the ticket. Wendy discovered this firsthand. "This travel agent got me the requisite ticket from Agra to Delhi. He told me it was the super-deluxe train; air-conditioned, the whole works. It wound up being hard benches with no assigned seats. I found out later that he had given me a $2 ticket to the 'cattle car' and kept the extra rupees."

After being told by my hotel in Varanasi that no tickets were available on trains from Siliguri (near Darjeeling) to Kolkata on the day I wanted to travel, I went to the train station to book it myself. I was pleasantly surprised to have one agent walk me through my options at a help desk and then point me to the foreign tourist office where I waited in air-conditioning to make the purchase. I was actually able to find a sleeper berth on the date that I wanted. Persistence always pays off in India!

If there is no official tourist booking office at the train station and your only option is to book your tickets like a local, there is a process to follow. You must first determine your train's number, either at the information booth, on a large reader board at the train office, online or in the *Trains at a Glance* timetable. Once you know which train you want, visit the information window to inquire if there is a seat available in the class you want. If so, you then visit the booking window designated for women and foreigners. There are fewer (and less aggressive) visitors to this window, taking some of the pain out of the process.

Some cities do have satellite booking offices so you don't have to go directly to the train station, but I have yet to find a guidebook listing their locations. I only know this fact because I have had Indian friends take me to one in Delhi. You might be lucky enough to stumble upon one of these, or try asking at your hotel for the nearest location.

Once, and only once, was I able to book a train ticket using the government's website (www.indianrail.gov.in). I booked it while in the U.S. using a credit card from a U.S. bank. While I was in India, however, I was never able to book it this way again and have heard similar reports of sporadic service from other travelers as well. Indian-based websites usually do not accept foreign-issued credit cards (though there is an effort to change this). If you have an Indian friend you're visiting, you might be able to use his or her card for booking.

Rail Passes — If you plan to travel regularly by rail, consider purchasing an Indrail Pass, available to foreigners and non-resident Indians. Good for unlimited travel for up to 90 days, it allows you to make and cancel reservations without a penalty. Though it doesn't guarantee a reservation, it may serve as an entrée on trains that are full. You can purchase a pass at any major rail station in India.

Tatkal Tickets — A *tatkal* (meaning "immediate" in Hindi) fare is a ticket issued to passengers who need to book their seat at the last minute — 10 percent of all seats are reserved for this special quota, and it works well on popular routes that sell out months in advance. Tickets can be booked no farther out than five days prior to departure, and they must be purchased directly from the departing station. With *tatkal* tickets you pay for the entire journey of that train (from Bangalore to Mumbai, for example), so it won't make economic sense if you're traveling a shorter distance on the same route (such as from Hospet to Pune).

Express Trains — These air-conditioned deluxe trains include luxuries such as videos, bottled water, meals, tea and snacks as well as soothing music. The routes are limited to connections between major cities and are the fastest trains available.

Deluxe Trains — There are several luxury trains catering to tourists. The Palace on Wheels (www.palaceonwheels.net) is run by Indian Railways. Tours start at $2,500 (based on double occupancy) for a one-week trip through Delhi, Rajasthan and Agra. Most (but not all) expenses are included.

Susan Foster, author of *Smart Packing for Today's Traveler,* loved her experience on the Palace on Wheels. "The Palace trip is the equivalent of going on a cruise — unpack once and your accommodations travel with you. Each day we stopped at a new city/destination and local tour guides and buses took us to all of the sites in that area. We found the guides excellent and the itineraries interesting. For me as an individual, trying to plan and organize all that was included in this trip would have been extremely difficult. I would not have been able to fill the days as effectively as they did. The trip was expensive but worth every cent."

Other options from Indian Railways include the Fairy Queen and the Royal Orient, with less expensive and less luxurious tours. There's also Deccan Odyssey (a joint venture with Indian Railways, the Taj Group of hotels and the Maharashtra Tourism Development Corporation) and Heritage on Wheels (created by the Indian government in response to the Palace on Wheels's success).

↭ Rapid Transit

After a day of shopping near Connaught Place in Delhi, I asked a taxi driver how much he would charge for a ride back to my guesthouse in northern Delhi. He shrugged, clearly not wanting to make the trip, and suggested that I take the metro instead. I figured if a guy in the transportation business was making the suggestion, there had to be something to it.

Delhi and Kolkata both have elevated and underground metro trains that carry passengers throughout the city. After my exchange with the taxi driver, I discovered that these rapid-transit systems are clean, cheap, fast, clean and safe — and did I mention clean?

At the Delhi metro, which opened in the early 2000s, you purchase a token (for single journeys), a Tourist Card (for unlimited travel over a short time period) or a Smart Card (for commuters) at a ticket window and then use the fully automated turnstiles for entering and exiting the platforms. Ticket agents are quite open to helping you through the process.

The Kolkata metro is a bit older, having opened in 1995. It allows you to ride nearly 10 miles for just eight rupees (less than 20 cents). It's a far more pleasant ride than the crowded inner-city buses and black-smoke-spewing auto-rickshaws. This citywide system provides magnetic tickets good for a set number of rides. Tickets are inserted into the turnstiles for entrance to and exit from the platforms.

While this form of rapid transit is a little intimidating at first, I wouldn't make my way through either of these cities without using these convenient modes of transportation.

Bangalore is scheduled to open their rapid-transit system by late 2011.

~ Domestic Flights

India has seen a proliferation of low-cost air carriers in recent years as locals have begun to travel more for both business and pleasure and tourism has increased. Take advantage of these flights if you need to cover a long distance and have the money but not the time (or inclination) to travel by train or bus.

Wendy traveled with Jet Airways for the first time from Delhi to Cochin. She liked the service so much that she figured out how to use it more frequently. "During my second time in India, I bought a Jet Airways [www.jetairways.com] pass where you could go to many cities for one cheap fare. It was a good deal, but changing tickets cost quite a bit and in some cases the bus was more convenient. I recommend planning your route in advance to take full advantage of the cost savings of the pass."

Newer airlines like Kingfisher Airlines (www.flykingfisher. com) have an excellent reputation and a fleet of spotless planes with meal and snack services. Even the airlines with aging fleets are no worse than low-cost carriers in the U.S.

No matter the airline, delays are frequent, particularly for routes in and out of Delhi during winter, when fog is an issue. I spent eight hours at the Chennai airport when my connecting flight was delayed out of Delhi.

Hot Tip! To avoid delays, book early-morning direct flights whenever possible.

Where and How to Book — The site Make My Trip (www. makemytrip.com) searches across full-service and low-cost carriers to provide the best prices on both domestic flights and those between India and the U.S., U.K. and Australia. Make My Trip also offers deals on hotels, rail tours and tour packages.

Cleartrip (www.cleartrip.com) specializes in flights and hotels within India. Special offers are listed on their home page. This site also provides train information.

These two sites offer comparable pricing. At this time, neither site accepts credit cards from foreign banks when booking within India, though this may be changing. In the meantime, if you have an Indian friend with a credit card, you can book online with his or her help. Note that fees and taxes can easily triple the base fare of the quoted ticket price. Pay attention to the final cost before booking.

If you're unable to book directly through one of these websites, make your reservations through a local travel agent. Their fees will vary greatly. I check the cost of my preferred flight(s) on one of the above sites and then shop around for the agent that will give me the closest price.

What to Expect — Due to India's size, air travel makes sense for longer distances, if it fits your budget. However, delays caused by fog or other weather-related issues means you could literally be stuck in your departure city for days.

Hot Tip! If you must be somewhere on a specific day — to catch your flight home, let's say — be sure to pad plenty of extra time into your flight schedule.

Compared to rail travel, flying can be expensive and potentially eat into your precious sightseeing time. For example, taking an overnight train from Delhi to Varanasi would be a better use of your time and money than flying, and it would allow you to save on a night's hotel stay.

It does little good to confirm your flight's departure time before arriving at the airport. Information is not always accurate and departure times change without notice. I waited for six hours at the Pune airport for a flight to Ahmedabad. There was no explanation for the delay and no one could be sure when the flight would depart. As a consolation, all waiting passengers received free tea and lunch snackpacks — better service than in the U.S.!

Any bags you are checking must first be x-rayed by your airline before you proceed to the ticket counter. A security tag or strap will be placed on the bag. Carry-on bags are screened separately before you proceed to the gate.

Airlines have become painfully tight with regards to the amount of luggage you're allowed to check and carry on. Research your airline's weight and baggage limits in advance. This is often printed on your ticket but can also be found on the airline's website. Pack accordingly and have a printout of the airline's rules with you when you check in. I suggest this because once when I was departing from Delhi, the British passengers checking in ahead of me ran into some issues. Though they had called in advance about the airline's weight limit, they were told one thing over the phone and another thing when they checked in. They had to pay more than $150 in charges because they exceeded their weight limits.

❧ Bus

Tourist buses are "deluxe" coaches run by private companies and may include air-conditioning and comfy high-backed seats. They generally run between the larger cities and popular destinations. Quality varies greatly and there's no way to confirm in advance how good (or bad) your coach will be. You might find it noisy if the video monitor is cranking out Bollywood hits and the trip can easily be slowed if the bus breaks down.

In complete contrast to this more expensive option are the government-owned buses that are used both within cities and for longer journeys. Service is frequent and extends far beyond the reaches of the railway line. They are also far less comfortable and reliable than either the tourist buses or trains.

Expect to share the ride with chickens, car engines, elderly women puking into plastic bags and screaming children. You may find yourself sitting on a hard bench with no breeze because the window either doesn't open or it's blocked by the other passengers. While tourist buses stow your bags under the carriage, on these cheaper buses you can often keep your bags with you, though you may end up sitting on them to save space. You may also have to relinquish them to the bus's roof (a dicey proposition).

There are areas, such as the Himalayas, where neither trains nor planes can reach, so the bus will be your only option.

Hot Tip! Lock the zippers shut on all of your bags when traveling by bus. If there's no room to store them inside the bus, you may be separated from them when they're relegated to the roof or under-carriage.

Where and How to Book — For tourist bus travel, book in advance through a ticketing agent, tour company or your hotel. In larger cities, these agents will advertise popular routes on sandwich boards, posters and in their office windows.

The public buses run frequently and tickets can be purchased just prior to your trip at the local bus station. Arrive at your bus early to secure a seat, otherwise you risk sitting on the floor or standing. Look for the ladies' queue in the bus station for quicker service.

∾ Cars and Drivers for Hire

Rentals — While it's possible, I wouldn't recommend renting a self-drive car in India. The roads are terrible and other drivers are insane. The smaller your vehicle, the more likely you are to be passed, pushed aside and taken over on the roadway. You'll also be dodging the throngs of cows, people, pushcarts, trucks, motorbikes, bicycles and horse-drawn carts that "share" the highways.

Jessica visited Mysore to study yoga for two months with a master. She quickly learned what she calls "The Hierarchy of the Road." Beginning with the most important, here is her list:

1. Cows
2. Buses
3. Trucks
4. Cars
5. Rickshaws
6. Motorcycles
7. Bicycles
8. People

"Drivers will do anything in their power to go around a cow even if it means running over a person." She adds, "I felt safer on a bike than walking because pedestrians are on the bottom of the list."

Nina, an Italian New Yorker to the core, travels to India yearly and loves its frenetic pace. "Chaos is normal. People don't stop at traffic lights so India is like Italy on steroids."

Hiring a Driver — It's far less harrowing (although probably not by much), and not very expensive, to hire a car and driver.

Where to Book — Hiring a car and driver is similar to just renting a car. You can book through an international or local car rental agency (Sixt is popular), but it's the driver who is responsible for the condition of the car when returned, not you. This can cost as little as $12 for day tours around a city like Delhi or Mumbai. You can also hire a driver for longer trips between cities for about $20 per day. The price is generally based on a per-kilometer cost and whether you're going to make use of the air-conditioning. Ask around or check a website like India Mike for recommendations for both international rental companies and local drivers to contact directly. Once you arrive, you'll notice there's no shortage of drivers willing to offer their services.

What to Expect — Jessica arranged for a driver to meet her at the Bangalore airport upon her arrival in India. "It was so worth the $50 to have someone pick me up and bring me to Mysore. It was easy and I felt so much safer than trying to figure out logistics on my own. I feel more vulnerable if I don't know what I'm doing and this helped me get there safely."

For day trips, make note of the mileage before you depart and confirm whether air-conditioning is included. Also write down the agreed-upon price. A verbal agreement can easily change at the end of the day when a disappointed driver realizes he wasn't able to make commission off of you from a shopping spree. After a full day of touring in Delhi, my driver insisted that we drove more than the 80 kilometers that were part of the package. Not knowing I had this limit to begin with, I argued that there was no possible way to drive 80 kilometers in a day given Delhi's traffic. I left him with the agreed-upon fare and no tip.

For longer journeys, expect to be barreling down highways at ungodly speeds, swerving to miss potholes, cows, dogs and anything else that has the nerve to get in your driver's way. He may believe it's simply karma if you get into an accident. Listen to your Western sensibilities and do not hesitate to ask him to slow down.

Hot Tip! On multiday trips, the driver will sleep in the car. Don't be fooled into giving him money for a hotel (or food, for that matter) unless this has been negotiated into the price from the beginning.

With the exception of the new superhighways, the roads are atrocious. Potholes are common and accidents are frequent. Only half of the country's roads are surfaced and only 4 percent measure up to international road standards.

Large rocks (rather than flares or orange cones) are placed in the middle of the highway to divert traffic away from an accident. You're then forced into oncoming lanes, making the other side of the road now two-way traffic. Even the new roads pose problems as drivers have increased their speed, causing more severe accidents than previously.

Avoid traveling by car at night on highways. Although there is less traffic, cows, bicyclists and pushcarts aren't equipped with headlights, making the probability of an accident exponentially greater when the sun goes down.

In cities, cars maneuver so close to each other in traffic that often the side-view mirrors collide. Even then, motorbikes, pedestrians and hawkers, selling everything from newspapers to flowers to dish towels, will make their way between vehicles at stop lights.

In the countryside, you'll be slowed by herds of goats and cows rambling down the road with their herder. Crops are often placed in the middle of the street to dry. Horse- and cow-drawn carts meander along as well.

Hand and horn signals are used to alert other drivers for various reasons. When a driver wants someone in front of him to move, he'll simply honk his horn. That alerts the driver in front to move over. He will then either wave his hand up and down out the window if it's unsafe to pass or will put on his own blinker if it's OK.

Seat belts are only required in certain larger cities, but they rarely work. If you have a working seat belt, use it, as it's one thing you can do to help minimize injury in the case of an accident.

Mobs of Indians will descend upon the scene of an accident and take matters into their own hands if someone they know has been hurt. Whether your driver is really at fault or not, with a foreigner in a car it may be assumed that your driver caused the accident. Lock yourself in your car if an angry group of Indians appears and wait for the police to arrive. However, when they do, never give your original passport (only a copy) to them or anyone else under these circumstances.

It's cheap to repair a vehicle but the process will surely be slow and the fix may not last long. Parts may be cobbled together because new parts are unavailable or too expensive for the locals to afford.

Hot Tip! If you ship your own vehicle to India, you'll need a carnet de passage issued by your embassy or consulate, which must be obtained prior to your arrival. This documentation proves that you didn't sell the vehicle while you were in the country or that you paid the required taxes if you did sell it.

∾ In-City Taxis

Though still cheap by Western standards, taxis are your most expensive option for moving about a city. On the plus side, they usually have air-conditioning and, when the windows are shut, allow you to be sealed off from both the pollution and beggars.

Though you may be told that it doesn't work, request that the meter be used. If you don't use a meter, inquire up-front what the cost of the trip will be and bargain hard for a good fare. Ask at your hotel what you should expect to pay to your destination so you'll have a starting point for bargaining.

If you're traveling at night, it's best to share a taxi with someone else. Even drivers double up for their own protection. Nina spends a lot of time in India's cities and still doesn't like this. "Taxi drivers in Delhi are always accompanied by another guy at night and I don't feel safe to be in a car with two guys. They'll make conversation and are just as nice but I'm just not comfortable."

The first time I saw tanks in the trunk of my taxi I was a bit alarmed, thinking we were carrying straight-up gas. I soon learned that these were for compressed natural gas, which taxis are now required to use in most cities. This effort has been a tremendous boon to cutting down on pollution.

Hot Tip! There are fixed-price taxi and rickshaw stands at airports and train and bus stations. The price is fair and you don't have to worry about bargaining with a group of drivers.

↶ Rickshaws

Auto-Rickshaws — These are really quite fun for buzzing around a city. Cheaper than taxis, they allow you to experience the elements. You'll sense the heat, breathe the pollution and dust, and feel the begging hands of street children. You'll also be exposed to the sounds of the busy roads, smell food cooking from outdoor vendors and hear the beating drums of street performers. Because you are so exposed, keep your personal items close to you so as to thwart any would-be thieves.

Nina relishes the experience. "I like to travel by rickshaw because you get to experience the sights and smells that you don't get in an air-conditioned taxi. And, because the rickshaw drivers don't speak English we'll speak a few words and then I can just enjoy the view."

Rickshaws generally have meters but I've yet to see a driver use one (at least for a tourist). Agree on a fare up-front so there are no surprises at the end of your journey. In Jaipur, I ran into an interesting twist. My driver suggested I "pay what I want" at the end of the day. Savvy. He knew that my guilt-ridden, overzealous rich pockets would shell out more than he would ever ask. Fortunately, two travelers told me what a fair price would be for the day. I therefore felt confident that I would neither under- nor overpay him.

Cycle-Rickshaws — In Varanasi, my train was departing sometime after 9 p.m. I had a cycle-rickshaw driver pick me up at my hotel to bring me to the station. Just as we were leaving, the power went out in our section of the city, including all of the street lights. It was pitch dark. I remembered that I had my flashlight in my jacket pocket. I pulled it out and shone it in the street just in front of the rickshaw's wheel. It lit up our way through half of the journey before the power went back on. The driver was very appreciative and the neighbors all laughed.

Several cities have cycle-rickshaws where young boys and pencil-thin gentlemen do their best at plying you through the streets. Slow-paced, methodical and quiet, it's actually quite a lovely way to get around.

I do have a twinge of guilt knowing how difficult this job is and how poor these drivers are. However, I also feel that this is all the more reason to use their services and help put some rupees in their pockets.

Pedi-Rickshaws — In Kolkata, there are many rickshaw drivers who pull their customers by foot (meaning they have no motor or bicycle). This is actually quite a sad sight. The city no longer issues permits for this sort of transportation so eventually this will die out, but for now you can still see this primitive form of transportation being used.

⌁ Bicycles

Don't let the fact that bicycles are so close to the bottom of the road hierarchy dissuade you from pedaling your way around the country.

India is home to the second-largest bicycle industry in the world. More than 12 million bikes are sold annually and include a wide range of cycles from mountain bikes to rickshaws. It's really quite feasible to land in India and purchase a bike for your travels.

However, it might be far more practical to ship your own bike — one that you are comfortable riding and for which you are properly outfitted. You can do this by using a premade bicycle box from CrateWorks (www.crateworks.com), or ask your local bike shop for help in shipping. Airlines will charge you an additional luggage fee for a bicycle; the amount varies from airline to airline.

᪥ Motorcycles

While in Sarnath, I met an adventurous Italian couple, Simone and Sebastian, heading south on a Chinese-built motorcycle with a sidecar. They were savoring every moment of their journey and pacing themselves by stopping for cups of chai every hour or so. The bike was adorned with a colorful painting of Ganesh, but their outlook was so delightful that I'm certain they were blessed by all the gods on their trip. They planned to ride for six months.

Many other travelers have forged a similar path on bikes purchased in India, such as an Enfield, or on their own bike, by which they've traveled overland or that they had shipped to the country. As a rider myself, I know the allure of being able to connect with the local culture and environment on a motorcycle. Being so exposed to the elements, you're able to smell not only cooking chapatis but cow poop as well. You're also an instant celebrity in every village or city, particularly as a woman, making it easy to meet locals and other travelers.

A motorcycle is agile enough to get you out of potentially hazardous road situations. The law requires that only the driver wear a helmet, but don't let this discourage you from wearing

৯৯৯ Connie's Story ৯৯৯

I had the idea to ride a motorcycle while traveling across Turkey on a bus a few years before I arrived in India. Then, when in India I saw the Enfield Bullet and remembered my dream of riding a motorcycle, so I bought one. I was working in Delhi as an editor for a wire service. When that contract ended, I knew it was time to set out to see India at my own pace.

I came back to the States for a visit and took the Motorcycle Safety Foundation course and learned how to ride.

I had to have a lot of faith and I had to have a plan. I first went to study the language to learn pronunciations and the names of towns so I wouldn't be sent off in the wrong direction.

With the help of a friend, I bought a 350 Enfield and had it up-graded with better brakes and boxes that locked. The bike cost about $1,200 to $1,400 new. The Enfields are simple, sturdy and durable. They are great for the roads but they need constant work.

In the U.S., front and rear brakes are operated with the right hand and foot, and the gears and clutch are operated with the left hand and foot. But Indian bikes are operated the opposite way. I had to relearn my skills.

Anyone with a screwdriver and hammer considers himself a mechanic in India but I wasn't OK with that. I studied with a mechanic who taught me how to fix everything. Even if I couldn't do it myself, I could at least stand over them to make sure they were doing it right in terms of the oil and changing the filters. And they weren't always happy about it.

As I rode, people thought I was a man but they knew I was a foreigner. Once it became obvious that I was a woman, it was great. I would get the thumbs up. The women would be drawn to me as well as the men.

In Rajasthan, I took off my helmet and there was a group of women standing outside. These tribal women were all looking over at me. Their faces were tattooed and they had all these bangles, and I was the odd one. They would touch themselves and then touch me to see if we were the same. The men moved back and gave space for us to interact.

There was one time when something was going wrong with the bike. I thought it was the chain because it kept jerking but I couldn't figure it out. I stopped in a small village. I was there working on the motorcycle and collecting this crowd that started with a few men. Then more people gathered, including a lot of women.

As I was packing up and ready to go, this woman had gone back to her house to get soap so that I could wash up. She didn't have a lot of money and she took it upon herself to help out. It was a small gesture that really stuck with me and meant a lot to me.

The human connection is so strong between cultures that people will know that you need help even if you don't share a language.

one as a passenger. Gloves, pants and a jacket are also necessary protective gear.

If you know what you're doing, you can purchase a reasonably priced motorcycle in India. A locally made bike will be easier to have fixed than a foreign-made bike. Check out motorcycle shops or repair centers to purchase a bike for sale by a local. Try hotels, hostels or restaurants for one that's for sale by another traveler.

❧ Boats and Ferries

Boats and ferries run among India's major islands, the Andaman & Nicobar Islands to the east and Lakshadweep to the west. Ferry runs are infrequent and long (every two weeks to Andaman & Nicobar and take about 60 hours) so you'll need to plan accordingly. Ferries also run in Mumbai's harbor where you can visit Elephanta Island.

You would think that in a country surrounded by beautiful coastline, sailing opportunities would abound. Unfortunately, India's infrastructure is not yet set up to accommodate this luxury, though it is possible to find tours that specialize in sailing from a few locations in Goa, Tamil Nadu and Kerala.

To experience India 's "backwaters," you can stay on a houseboat in Kerala or simply try traveling through the southern part of the state on one of the passenger boats.

LODGING OPTIONS

YOU'LL *be faced with many challenges during your travels in India. Having a place to retreat to and where you can get a restful night of sleep will help you face the day refreshed and with patience. This doesn't mean that you have to budget the majority of your money for your accommodations, but that it's worth being choosy so you can be comfortable.*

ᨆ Some Helpful Guidelines

Always check out the room before you pay up front or agree to stay. Check for mosquitoes, mosquito nets, hot water and the cleanliness of the sheets. As a woman traveler, you should pay special attention to the reliability of the locks on both the doors and windows. If anything is lacking but you're still willing to stay there, use it as a bargaining chip to bring down the price.

Even if a proprietor insists that a room has hot water, you may discover that this really isn't the case or that there *may* be hot water for an hour or so each day, when it's shared by all guests. I have found that sometimes you need to let the water run for 5 or 10 minutes before the hot water kicks in. While this kills my sense of water preservation, it may be the only way to take a hot shower.

For every hotel, including high-end accommodations, you can negotiate: ask for a better price or a room upgrade, or see if you can get a discount if you pay cash or stay more than one night. Simply asking may get you a better room or lower rate.

The presence of an air-conditioner in a room doesn't mean that it works. If temperatures are high, make sure the room has a working air-conditioner or fan.

Hot Tip! Most showers are equipped with what's called a geyser. This tank, often perched high up in the shower, must be turned on to heat the shower water. A green light denotes that the water is hot.

Hotel touts enthusiastically (and aggressively) meet you at railway and bus stations or at the airport in order to direct you to available accommodations. See Chapter 3, Culture Shock, for information on dealing with these touts.

Personally, I prefer to book my hotel in advance (mid-range accommodations generally have a website with contact information listed) and arrange for a driver to pick me up when I arrive in a city. I then don't have to worry about the stress of bargaining with touts and rickshaw drivers. Rarely do you have to provide a credit card to hold a room. If you don't like the hotel or room once you arrive, don't be shy about moving to another location. Consult your guidebook or rely on a rickshaw driver — there will most likely be one circling the hotel looking for a fare.

∿ Budget Accommodations

There's no shortage of cheap accommodations in India. Whether it's a hotel or someone's home that's been converted into a guesthouse, you can easily find a room with shared bath for as little as a few dollars per night. Hostel-style dorm rooms in the off-season will be even cheaper.

Check the Youth Hostels Association of India website (www.yhaindia.org) for a complete listing of affiliated hostels. Prices range from $6 to $20 per night depending on the location. There are also a few hostels that are part of the Hostelling International (www.hihostels.com) network.

Unlike countries in the West, you don't have to rely on youth hostels for an inexpensive bed. Most cities and villages with any sort of tourist draw will have guesthouses in the budget range. In Delhi, I've stayed at the Wongdhen House in the Majnu-ka-Tilla Tibetan refugee village several times. It's close to a metro stop but far enough away from the city center so as to actually be relaxing. Rooms average about $10 per night. Guidebooks and online resources can help you find these sorts of options.

7. LODGING OPTIONS

Hot Tip! Bring a sleepsack, like the ones made by Cocoon (www. cocoonusa.com), or have one made upon arrival. You'll feel a lot more comfortable sleeping in your own bag rather than in a hotel's sheets and blankets (which aren't always washed after use).

You'll want to carry your own towel or sarong to use for bathing, as budget accommodations don't always offer this perk.

⌀ Homestays

The real fun in budget accommodations is found through programs like Servas (www.servas.org), Couchsurfing (www. couchsurfing.com), GlobalFreeloaders (www.globalfreeloaders.com) and Hospitality Club (www.hospitalityclub.org). Through these organizations you can connect with the locals and find a willing host with whom you can stay for free.

Servas is an international nongovernmental multicultural organization dedicated to fostering world peace, mainly by connecting travelers with potential hosts. Participants are pre-screened by an interviewer and the yearly membership fee is $85. In addition, there is a small refundable fee to obtain the printed list of hosts in the countries you are visiting. Lists include the number of people that can be hosted and for how long, as well as what languages are spoken in the home.

I stayed with a Servas host in Sarnath and met some really lovely people. My host was a German woman who had lived in India for 17 years and was married to an Indian man. Her quiet home was a sanctuary from the busy life of Varanasi just 30 minutes away, and she served the most wonderful breakfasts, complete with homemade sweet breads.

As a solo woman traveler, Margie made a lasting connection with her Servas hosts in a remote area of India. "I went to the village in the north because I made a Servas connection. There were no other tourists there. I work as a health-care professional and chose these hosts because they were doctors and because they spoke English. These people were so generous and interesting to talk to. We discussed many topics and, among other things, they convinced me of the merits of arranged marriages."

Couchsurfing, GlobalFreeloaders and Hospitality Club are three online options that also connect travelers with potential hosts. As in the case of Servas, no money changes hands, though it's in good taste to provide your host with a small gift or to perhaps treat them to a meal.

With these free services, both travelers and hosts create online profiles, which have feedback areas where you can see what other travelers and hosts have said about each other. In my experience, the Couchsurfing website has more active participants, making it easier to find accommodations. However, some people belong to only one of these sites, so check all three.

Stephanie spent many of her nights with Couchsurfing hosts and enjoyed the company since she was on her own. "I would have been lonelier if I wasn't staying with families. In Varanasi, I was with a family that included five daughters. They would henna my hands and accompany me sightseeing because they hadn't seen everything in the area. On my birthday, the mother made a special dinner for me. I always felt safe and well cared for."

I never request a stay unless it is with a woman or the woman is the primary contact (as with my host in Sarnath). Admittedly, this is difficult in India because it is such a male-dominated society. Always read over the reviews by other travelers and contact them directly with specific concerns before staying with a host. Never stay with a single man in India.

7. LODGING OPTIONS

Hot Tip! Servas hosts are prescreened and Couchsurfing monitors all emails that are exchanged via the website. Therefore, you may feel more comfortable staying with a host from one of these two programs over the others.

In all likelihood, you will have made contact via email with your potential host no matter which program you used to find them. When possible, you should also chat by phone to get to know them better prior to your arrival. If you have any doubt about the arrangement, go with your gut and stay elsewhere.

If you choose a homestay option, be prepared to live like the locals, using squat toilets and eating with your right hand. The families participating may or may not have servants to clean the house or cook. Offering to cook a dish from home can be a fun way to introduce your culture and lifestyle to your hosts.

Sleeping arrangements will vary in all of these cases and will be included in the description written by the host. Possibilities range from space on a floor, a couch or your own private bedroom.

Some people in these programs are open to simply getting together for coffee or a meal. This would be a great way to meet the locals but still have the comfort and privacy of your own hotel room.

❧ *Gurudwaras* and *Dharmashalas*

Both *gurudwaras*, places of worship for Sikhs, and *dharmashalas* (or *dharamshala*), places of worship for Buddhists, Muslims and Jains, offer free or low-cost accommodations for travelers and pilgrims. When there is no charge, a donation is greatly appreciated.

Accommodations and rules vary greatly. The facility may ban alcohol, drugs, smoking, meat or music. *Gurudwaras* (the most famous of which is the Golden Temple in Amritsar) require that a woman wear a headscarf, and in all temples you should avoid wearing shorts or short-sleeve shirts.

Search online for these accommodations or ask at a local temple once you arrive in town.

❧ Mid-Range Hotels

Jon and I arrived in Udaipur after a long taxi ride from Ahmedabad. We targeted an area of town near the lake that looked interesting and centrally located. While Jon waited in the taxi with our luggage, I walked around to the various guesthouses, finally striking a bargain ($12 per night) with the proprietors of a little family-run hotel. We had a view of the Lake Palace from built-in window seats, a private bath and a mosquito net for the king-size bed.

For just $10 to $30 you can find a comfortable room most anywhere in India with private bath, Western toilet, mosquito net, hot water, television, telephone, room service, air-conditioning or fan and a view.

Your guidebook will list the more popular options (though prices tend to rise when a hotel makes it into a guidebook), but a simple online search can turn up lots of additional choices. Unless you're visiting a destination during a festival — anywhere during *Diwali,* or Pushkar during the Camel Fair, for example — you should be able to book a hotel just days in advance of your arrival, giving you plenty of flexibility in your schedule.

✧ Bed-and-Breakfasts

I stayed at the Home Away from Home in Delhi in a wonderful gated community and, despite the cigarette smoke that snuck under my bedroom door, I loved the chance to stay with a local woman. Breakfast was even served by the live-in servant.

A bed-and-breakfast in India, you ask? You bet! In late 2006, the Ministry of Tourism launched a program to help alleviate the shortage of hotels and guesthouses available in Delhi in preparation for the 2010 Commonwealth Games. Under this program, homeowners can offer up to 5 rooms or 10 beds in their home to tourists and must include a continental breakfast for all guests.

Whether it's in Delhi or elsewhere in the country, a bed-and-breakfast stay is an affordable option (rates aren't much more than a mid-range hotel) and allows you to meet local residents and get a feel for how they live without sleeping on their couch ☺. It's a financial boon for proprietors and it allows them to meet people from all over the world.

Mangosteen (www.bednbreakfasthomes.com), based in Delhi, is a company that markets bed-and-breakfasts in India. Co-owner Sumitra Senapaty explains, "The B&Bs have all been inspected for their suitability for different segments of travelers, this includes vegetarians and single ladies traveling on work." Mangosteen matches up their customers with the appropriate host to maximize security and meet the needs of the traveler. They currently offer accommodations in Delhi and Jaipur but have plans to expand.

✧ Heritage Hotels

On occasion, upgrading to nicer accommodations for a night is well worth it. Sigrid traveled with a group of women friends and discovered this for herself. "Depending on your budget, periodically plan on a nicer hotel that's clean. And, stay away from a city — India is much more intense than anything you can imagine."

Palaces, estates and aristocratic homes that were once part of the British Raj era have been turned into heritage hotels. This has been one way to help owners preserve these royal home-steads, which can be costly to maintain. Carolyn was part of a tour group to India. "Many of the places where we stayed were maharajas'palaces that were turned into hotels. Every one of them was beautiful and a great experience. The food was deli-cious and beautifully prepared."

The vast majority are located in Rajasthan, though there are many peppered throughout the country, from Goa to Pondicherry. Don't expect a bargain. While this is at the up-per end of the scale, rooms at the Lake Palace Hotel in Udaipur start at about $800.

❧ High-End Hotels

Though I'm a big fan of luxury now and then, the more expen-sive the accommodations, the further away you'll be from the people and culture. Enticed by the private pool, grand buffet breakfast, satellite TV and newspaper delivered to your room, you'll have little desire to step out into a city's hectic streets for a dose of genuine India.

Well-known international and India-based chain hotels are available. Compared to similar services and accommodations in the West, the price may be a bargain, but they are quite ex-pensive by Indian standards. A basic room can easily cost $500, and prices are usually quoted in U.S. dollars.

7. LODGING OPTIONS

⌾ Home Swaps

Staying in one place for an extended period of time allows you to have a deeper understanding of a destination than if you are constantly moving. Settling into someone's home, rather than staying in a hotel, will help develop this understanding even further.

There are resources online that connect people interested in a home swap; you find someone who wants to stay in your home while you stay in their home in India. This is an affordable option for families and it allows you to live amongst the locals.

Though there are several long-established companies that provide listings, Home Exchange (www.homeexchange.com) has the most extensive offerings in India.

⌾ Farmstays and Rural Visits

India's cities can be absolutely overwhelming due to the population, pollution and traffic. Getting away from the sheer numbers of people can be a salvation for anyone, whether you're used to a metropolis or not.

World Wide Opportunities on Organic Farms (WWOOF, www.wwoof.org) is an international movement that helps people share sustainable ways of living. Once you pay the $40 one-year membership fee, you are given a list of participating farms. You make direct arrangements with a host farm, and then provide them with light manual labor in exchange for accommodations and meals. Depending on the time of year, you may have no chores or you may spend four to six hours a day harvesting food. India joined WWOOF in early 2007.

If working for your accommodation isn't of interest but you would still like a rural experience, try Explore Rural India (www.exploreruralindia.org). This website provides information about and connects travelers with rural communities, including women's co-ops. Accommodations range from homestays to deluxe hotels.

❧ Craigslist

Yes, there's a Craigslist (http://geo.craigslist.org/iso/in) in India, and it's still called Craigslist. If you're planning an extended stay, check listings on this site. More than a dozen cities are included and you can search for vacation rentals, home sales and apartments for rent.

Of course you can always shop for jewelry or find a job on this site as well!

8.

FEASTING

I NDIA *is a gastronomical delight. Food varies greatly by region but you can be sure to experience plenty of flavorful vegetarian and nonvegetarian dishes throughout the country. No trip to the subcontinent would be complete if you didn't open yourself to the array of options offered in restaurants and hotels, from street vendors and in people's homes.*

❦ Types of Restaurants

There are several types of restaurants to be aware of, including *dhabas* and *bhojanalayas*; local, deluxe and tourist restaurants; and fast-food joints. Knowing the options will help create a more "full-filling" experience for you and your tummy.

Dhabas and *bhojanalayas* are inexpensive diners that are frequented by truck drivers and busloads of long-distance travelers. Found along busy highways, they may have a gas station attached. Offerings are basic but can be quite delicious, cheap and fresh. I've noticed that Café Coffee Days (the Indian equivalent of Starbucks) have been cropping up right next to these local eateries. They are a sterile alternative to a *dhaba* or *bhojanalaya,* serving premade sandwiches, cookies and espresso.

Walking through the streets of Bangalore, I followed my friends through an unmarked door, up a set of stairs and into the Krishna Café. The restaurant was filled with locals sopping up their curries with *dosas* and *idlis.* It was my first introduction to south Indian food and one of the most memorable (and tasty) restaurant meals I have had in India.

If you know where to find them, local restaurants like the Krishna can be one of the best options for authentic and inexpensive food. Often tucked away down a back alley or up a discreet set of stairs, these neighborhood favorites serve some of the most delightful cuisine you'll eat during your journey. Ask a local where she eats with her family or to suggest a restaurant that specializes in the food from that particular region.

Given India's growing middle class, it's no wonder that there is an increasing number of deluxe restaurants that serve authentic local cuisine catering to Indians but where foreigners are welcome. These can be found in five-star hotels and as independent restaurants in larger cities. Guidebooks generally list a few higher-end options and reservations may be required.

Tourist restaurants can be a treat if you're tired of the usual Indian fare or you're in need of some food that reminds you of home. Catering to Western tastes, their menus include macaroni and cheese, sandwiches, spaghetti and, for breakfast, banana pancakes, oatmeal and toast. With an upset stomach in Udaipur, I noshed on French fries and tomato soup, allowing my system to settle on these more familiar (and bland) foods.

Fast-food restaurants are, unfortunately, found in all the major cities. You won't find a beef burger at McDonald's, but they do serve Chicken Maharaja Macs and McVeggie Burgers. KFC, Pizza Hut and Domino's are also ubiquitous. In addition, there are local chain restaurants such as Nirula's.

❧ Eating with Your Right Hand

Eating in India can be tricky if you aren't familiar with the process. Meals are generally served with either chapatti or rice and come with a variety of curries or sauces used for dipping. You rip apart your chapatti with your right hand and gather these sauces and rice together in your bread, using your right hand to eat. Though silverware might be provided, Indians almost always use their right hand.

My biggest challenge in eating this way is in ripping apart the warm flatbread without the help of my left hand. Luckily, I've noticed other travelers, as well as Indians, struggling with this too.

Kaydin lived with several families during her year in India and had similar issues. "The most difficult part of eating was using one hand for breaking the chapatti. After a month, it was easier because I gained some strength in my hand." You may not have the opportunity to practice on three meals a day for a year like Kaydin, but doing your best will still impress the locals.

In restaurants frequented by tourists, the right-hand rule is a bit more relaxed and a fork and knife will usually be available.

Hot Tip! To combat the tendency to eat with your left hand, keep it tucked under your left leg so that you're not tempted to use it.

Other eating habits to avoid include: passing food with your left hand; double-dipping if you're sharing curries or sauces; and using your personal spoon or fork to dish out items from a communal bowl.

❧ Spices and Herbs

Our Indian friend Ramesh came to our home in Seattle to teach us a thing or two about Indian cooking. In a duffle bag he had packed an *idli* maker, blender, pressure cooker, rice, veggies, coconut milk, mango juice and a container of secret spices that his mother and sister in India had concocted. To our delight, this container of *sambar* powder got accidentally left behind with us! We coveted this exotic mix and sparingly doled it out in dishes for months.

According to Joan Peterson and Indu Menon in their guide *Eat Smart in India,* "Spices and herbs are the cornerstone of Indian cooking. Chefs and home cooks alike are well versed in the individual characteristics of each seasoning."

Step into an Indian kitchen and you'll find individual containers of cumin, coriander, mustard seeds, cardamom, mace, turmeric, nutmeg and more. Each meal is prepared with a special combination of these spices and herbs. It seems an inherent trait of Indians that they know exactly which spice gets added for an effect and in what order they should be added.

As a woman traveler, take advantage of any opportunity to visit the kitchen of a private home and ask about their spices. I'm sure your host will be delighted you've asked.

ᴥ Special Diets

Vegetarians, take heart. India is one of the easiest places in the world for you to enjoy a scrumptious meat-free meal. Restaurants advertise on their awnings or windows whether they serve veg, pure-veg (without eggs), non-veg or all types of meals. Dahl is nearly always available, making it easy to eat a protein-rich diet.

Though vegetarianism is popular, veganism is not. Many dishes include yogurt, *paneer* (cheese), ghee (clarified butter) and/or milk.

For those with allergies or other food sensitivities, eating could be more complicated. Sigrid must avoid certain ingredients and found that it was difficult to accommodate her needs. "I had no idea that it would be so difficult to eat in India because I don't eat wheat or dairy. They also use a lot of salt, which I have to watch in my diet."

Hot Tip! If you have special dietary requirements, stock up on snacks purchased at a market or grocery store so that you don't get caught without food if a restaurant cannot accommodate your needs.

ᴥ Complementary Foods

Indian meals are served as a variety of small dishes. Consuming complementary foods is borne out of the Ayurvedic tradition of balancing your *doshas* (see Chapter 9, Your Health, for more information on *doshas*) to keep your body in harmony. This combining of foods also provides an array of six tastes: pungent, astringent, salty, sweet, sour and bitter. An example of this balance is to eat spicy (hot) dishes with (cooling) yogurt.

For a sampling of many of these foods, try a *thali* plate, which includes dishes of chutneys, curries, dips, *raita* and dahl served on a large tray with a form of chapatti and perhaps rice. These are sometimes all-you-can-eat meals in which the waiter continuously fills up on any item that you are lacking.

ᴖ Regional Variety

If you're traveling to more than one region, you'll quickly come to realize that the dish you fell in love with in Kerala is difficult to find in Rajasthan. Take advantage of regional specialties that draw upon the abundance of the local spices, vegetables and meat, and don't be shy about experimenting.

Andrea realizes it's more difficult to be adventurous in your eating when you have a short amount of time in the country — you don't want to spend any of your precious days with stomach issues. However, for those traveling for three weeks or more, be daring like Andrea was. "I wanted to try everything. I didn't want to miss out on an experience by turning down an invitation for dinner."

ᴖ Fruits and Vegetables

In cities, you'll find a large variety of fruits and vegetables sold by vendors (such as those selling coconuts) or at small storefronts. In Bangalore, a line of locals could be found regularly at the newly opened juice shop. For less than a dollar, customers could order watermelon juice or banana or mango shakes. Cups of cut fruit are also available at these juice stands.

In villages, a vendor pushing a cart filled with items such as tomatoes, potatoes, carrots and apples may roam the streets selling door to door.

Hot Tip! Avoid watered-down fruit drinks or smoothies. Request milk instead since the water and/or ice might be contaminated.

❧ Sweets

In Agra, I tried a *jalebi* (fried batter dipped in syrup). It looked deceptively scrumptious, like a funnel cake dipped into orange-colored sweetness. It was so syrupy, however, that I couldn't eat more than two bites, and even that caused me to have a stomachache! I love sweets, but some Indian treats are a bit much for me.

Sweet shops and *jalebi* vendors dot streets throughout the country. There are also a fair number of bakeries that serve treats geared towards Western tastes. Croissants are particularly popular in French-influenced Pondicherry, but cakes and cookies can be found even in small villages like Hampi.

❧ Vendor Food

Food sold by vendors on the street is generally quite safe if it is prepared fresh and hot. The water used in many items, however, is unlikely to be filtered, and the oil used for frying may be recycled. Buy from stalls where the locals are eating and where the food appears fresh.

Laura joined a study-abroad program and spent a few months in Bangalore. Though most of her meals were prepared in her dorm, she knew she felt at home when she and her friend ordered from a street vendor. "We both downed our warm Fantas and then bought some sugar cookies. We could see ants on them and knew we had been in India a long time when we just brushed off the ants and ate the cookies."

Kaydin also learned what to eat and what to avoid. "Don't eat *pani puri* because you can't be sure the water is safe." She's right — these round, hollow fried crisps filled with potatoes and chili often contain mint water. "Food stalls in small towns may not look clean, but they are. If there are lots of people [eating there]... you know it's safe. Order something simple that's fried or cooked at a high temperature and nothing with lots of water in it."

⤳ Beverages

Sharing Drinks — Drinks may be shared, but you'll notice that a person's lips never actually touch the bottle or glass. Instead, Indians hold the container just above their mouth and adeptly pour. Any time I've tried this, I've ended up pouring the liquid down my chest!

Nonalcoholic Drinks — Chai is ubiquitous throughout India. This black tea with milk and sugar is flavored with cinnamon, cardamom and other delicious spices. Often served quite sweet, it is far tastier than anything I've tried at home. Chai wallahs on trains and street corners serve chai in tiny terra-cotta or plastic cups and restaurants serve it in small tin cups.

"Tea was critical to our trip," said Jennifer, who found that tea, more than anything, helped her to accept and adjust to the Indian way of life. "I would suggest having a large tea budget. When we were in Nainital, we would sit down and have tea and talk. I would have tea and write...tea helped me take in India more slowly."

Even given chai's ubiquity, coffee is becoming more popular. Shops such as Café Coffee Day and India Coffee House (which started in the 1950s) are starting to crop up in major cities and at rest areas on major highways.

In a hot country like India, you'll also want something to cool you down. For many years foreign soft drinks were banned, giving local companies the opportunity to build their brands. This changed in the early '90s and both Pepsi and Coca-Cola aggressively entered the market. Due to ongoing concerns about pesticides found in these products, these soft drinks are actually banned in some regions. The manufacturers deny that the levels found are dangerous to one's health and the battle rages on.

Hot Tip! Aspartame, used in diet soft drinks and other low-calorie food products, is carcinogenic and its toxicity is exacerbated when exposed to heat, as in warm climates. Avoid these products while in India as proper refrigeration and storage is rarely achered to.

A *lassi* is a blended yogurt drink, served in restaurants and by street vendors. With a slightly sour taste, it may also contain sugar, salt, fruit or spices such as cumin. Avoid those made with water and/or ice. A *bang lassi* is laced with marijuana and can be found on menus in popular tourist destinations.

For Westerners, fruit shakes are more popular than *lassis*. Order yours straight up or with milk rather than water.

Drink lots of water, especially if you're traveling in the heat. Bottled water is available everywhere, but I recommend purifying your own from the tap in order to cut down on garbage. See Chapter 9, Your Health, for more information on safe drinking water.

Alcohol — During dinner at a restaurant in Hampi (officially a dry town), patrons were offered drinks by the waiter.

He then drove to the next village, about 20 minutes away, to fill requests for beer and wine. In Varkala, Kerala, patrons are served alcohol in coffee mugs and their beers are placed in a paper bag on the ground.

Though prohibition is in effect in some regions, including the entire state of Gujarat (Gandhi's birthplace), alcohol may be served to tourists on the sly. You may notice "special" or "happy" drinks on the menu — these are laced with either alcohol or marijuana.

Beer is by far the drink of choice for most travelers as it's relatively inexpensive and widely available. Wine is becoming more popular as grape-growing regions near Mumbai and Bangalore are being developed. Though improving, the quality is not on par with Napa or Bordeaux and bottles are quite costly given the quality. Rarely is it served by the glass because there are just not enough customers to justify opening an entire bottle.

Never missing an opportunity to enter a growing market, foreign-based liquor companies are expanding distribution into India. Spirits are now readily available and, in some cases, bottled in-country. Prices are dropping so as to expand the reach.

Mixed drinks are available in specially designated bars, usually attached to a hotel. These bars are rarely frequented by women, especially women on their own, except in areas that are known for nightlife, such as Goa.

You may be offered locally manufactured alcohol such as toddy (palm wine) in Kerala, *taddy* in Bengal, or *chang* and *tumba* from the Tibetans. If you have a strong stomach and are adventurous, you may want to try these out.

YOUR HEALTH

STARTING *your trip as healthy and fit as possible will boost your immune system and help stave off the possibility of getting sick in India. There will be a lot of things working against you: pollution, sensation overload and the distance you'll be traveling simply to get to the country. Despite all this, you can still make your way through the subcontinent as a happy camper.*

◆ Health, Travel and Evacuation Insurance

I would never travel to India without insurance coverage for both health and evacuation provisions. I highly recommend both.

Did you get that? I **highly** recommend *both*!

Many insurance policies cover travel abroad in the case of an accident and may reimburse you for emergency and urgent-care expenses once you've paid out of pocket. Government programs such as Medicare, however, generally do not cover care outside of your country of residence. Check with your provider to confirm if and how much coverage you may have in India. If you do have coverage, keep in mind that it might not include activities such as adventure sports or riding a motorcycle.

Hot Tip! If your health insurance doesn't cover international travel, keep your insurance card with you anyway in the event you need it while traveling to and from your destination.

Evacuation insurance can ensure transportation to a medical facility in the case of a serious accident or illness for which you don't want to be treated by the local hospital. For example, you would want to be taken to Delhi, Bangkok or even home in the case of a severely broken bone caused by a fall or head injuries sustained in an accident. The cost of such an evacuation can easily top out at $60,000. With evacuation insurance, you would be responsible for your deductible and little, if anything, else.

In the past, I have taken out policies from both MEDEX (www.medexassist.com) and Medjet Assist (www.medjetassistance.com). Though I've never had to use either (thank goodness!), the process of signing up can be done in literally minutes. The cost is a fraction of the amount of your entire trip and minor compared to the potential out-of-pocket expenses that might be incurred in the case of an accident.

If you've shelled out a heap of money for a tour package or nonrefundable hotel or air tickets, consider travel insurance. For a relatively small fee, you'll be reimbursed in the event you have to cancel your trip. Depending on the policy, other benefits may include baggage reimbursement, as well as medical, dental and evacuation coverage. Visit Insure My Trip (www. insuremytrip.com) to compare prices from about 20 different providers.

↬ Medicines and Prescriptions

It's not unusual to have some health issues crop up while traveling in India. These might include allergic reactions, intestinal issues or other problems to which you must pay special attention.

Don't allow these issues to prevent you from traveling, but know your limitations and be prepared with remedies and medicines for your specific predispositions.

If you carry prescription drugs, keep them in their original packages and bring copies of the prescriptions. The copies will not only confirm your need for the medication if you're questioned by authorities, but you'll be able to get a refill if you run out or lose your bottle along the way.

Prepare a medical bio sheet that includes detailed info on your health, medications and allergies. Include the names and phone numbers for both your doctors and family members. Keep a copy at home as well as one in your luggage.

Hot Tip! If you have allergies or medical issues, wear a medical alert bracelet. In the event of an emergency, the information on the bracelet can help a doctor more quickly diagnose a problem or be sure you're given the correct medicine.

∿ Vaccinations

India does not have any vaccination requirements for entry. If you are arriving from a country considered a yellow fever zone, however, you will need proof that you have been vaccinated against it prior to arrival.

I limit my vaccinations to the bare minimum. This is due in part to my aversion to injecting my body with a foreign substance and in part to my fear of needles (if I were a junkie, I'd have to be tranquilized just to use them!).

Consult your doctor or a travel clinic well in advance of your travels, as some of these vaccinations are given as a series of shots over numerous months. Ask for a "yellow health card" and get a stamp for each vaccine that includes the dates you received them. This card will save you from unnecessary shots in the future and will be an easy guide to what you need for that next trip abroad. Consider it as important as your passport and keep it in a safe place.

There are a handful of vaccines I consider very important: the hepatitis vaccines and DPT.

Hepatitis — Hepatitis A is usually caused by contaminated food or water. It is the mildest version of hepatitis and is not chronic. This vaccine is given in a series of two shots and will protect you for at least 10 years.

Hepatitis B is passed on by unclean needles, blood transfusions, sex with an infected person or from mother to child

OTHER VACCINATIONS

In addition to the hepatitis and DPT vaccinations recommended in the text, consider the following vaccinations prior to your trip:

- **Polio** — Highly contagious and still found in the poorer regions of India.

- **Typhoid** — Spread through contaminated food or water, this is endemic to the area but rarely seen outside of the monsoon season.

- **Japanese B Encephalitis** — Highly fatal; rural India continues to have outbreaks of this mosquito-borne illness.

- **Meningitis** — Spread by airborne bacteria, this can be fatal. Outbreaks still occur in India.

- **Rabies** — Consider shots if you will be in remote areas where there are wild animals or dogs. You can also get a series of (painful) shots after being bitten by an animal suspected of carrying rabies.

- **Chicken Pox** — If you haven't already had chicken pox, consider the varicella vaccine to protect yourself from them.

- **Tuberculosis** — The Centers for Disease Control does not recommend a vaccine unless there is a possibility that you will spend a prolonged amount of time in an enclosed area with someone with TB.

- **Cholera** — Contracted through contaminated water or food, there is no vaccine available in the U.S. (though t is available in other countries). It's unlikely that a healthy person would show symptoms of this bacterium, which is endemic to the Ganges River.

in utero. It can be chronic and it's believed that anywhere from 500,000 to 1.2 million people die each year from hep B. Because you can't foresee the potential need for a blood transfusion, I recommend this vaccination, which is given in three shots over six months.

Hepatitis C is also passed on through blood transfusions and can be chronic, with symptoms that lie dormant for decades. There is no vaccine for hep C. My friend Norma died from hep C, which she acquired after a blood transfusion in Asia 30 years prior to the hepatitis emerging in her body. The best line of defense is to not allow a blood transfusion unless you are in a hospital with Western-trained doctors and facilities or until you can be evacuated to one.

DPT — This one shot covers diphtheria, pertussis and tetanus and must be updated at least every 10 years to remain effective. Diphtheria is a highly contagious upper respiratory infection. Pertussis, known as whooping cough, is also highly contagious and easily spread through coughing. Tetanus is contracted when a cut or open wound becomes infected — this can easily happen if you step on a dirty nail.

✤ Staying Healthy on the Flight

Liquids — It's a long flight to India from most points of departure. Do everything you can to remain healthy along the way, including staying hydrated. Drink a glass of water for every hour of flight and resist the temptation to drink alcohol and coffee (both of which can cause dehydration). This will help you thwart off airborne illnesses and keep you feeling better overall. If you have a small bladder, consider requesting an aisle seat so you aren't trapped when your seatmate falls asleep and you need to use the restroom.

Eating Healthily — Although airlines now provide lots of in-flight entertainment, flying can still be boring. The tendency is to eat just to have something to do. Pre-order a vegetarian or low-calorie meal, or resist the foil-covered tray altogether and instead bring your own healthful snacks such as fruit, nuts, seeds or protein bars. Since you'll be stationary for an extended period of time, portion them out so that you're eating a smaller amount than normal at each snack time. Better to eat a small bag of healthful snacks than a thousand calories of fat, grease, sugar and carbohydrates.

Exercise — Deep vein thrombosis (DVT) occurs when a blood clot forms in your leg after long periods of sitting still. It is potentially fatal to old and young alike if fragments of the clot move into your lungs To minimize your risk, purchase compression socks that reduce swelling and fatigue.

Stretching in your seat every hour or two also helps. Try the following: rotate your ankles, pump your feet up and down, bring your knees to your chest (one at a time), roll your shoulders and neck, and stretch your shoulders by crossing your arms across your chest one at a time. Also, take walks up and down the aisle. When I get up to use the restroom, I always take 15 minutes to stretch.

Jet Lag — Jet lag is caused by a change in your circadian rhythm, which is ultimately a disruption in the amount of light and dark to which you are exposed. When traveling across numerous time zones, your body gets out of sync with the time at your destination and literally becomes confused as to when to eat and sleep. While not usually debilitating, it can be annoying since you want to maximize your awake time while traveling.

Unless you're already in Asia, getting to and from India is a bear. Not usually prone to jet lag, I had a terrible time readjusting after returning from one trip. I attribute it to the excitement of having on-demand movies at my fingertips (after a month of Hindi-only films) on the seatback in front of me. I was so thrilled to be watching movies in English that I actually enjoyed *The Bourne Ultimatum* (not usually my genre), but sleeping probably would have been a better idea.

On top of the jet lag, I felt the culture shock of being back in the U.S., and I longed for Indian food, music and sights — I felt out of sorts for a month.

Besides turning off the in-flight entertainment system, there are a number of things you can do to help offset jet lag while you're on the plane.

First, set your watch to the local time and act accordingly. If it's the middle of the night in India, sleep and get rest. Set your alarm for "morning" so that you can get on track with the local time. Use natural sleep aids such as valerian root, eyeshades, earplugs or noise-canceling headphones and a travel pillow.

Drink lots of fluids to keep your body hydrated and eat well, avoiding airplane and airport food. Eat when you would normally eat based on the time at your destination.

No-Jet-Lag (www.nojetlag.com) is a homeopathic tablet that contains chamomile and is proven to be a safe and effective way to get over jet lag by inducing a light sleep. You can order this from their website or pick it up at your local pharmacy or grocery store.

Hot Tip! Avoid sleeping pills. You'll want to sleep lightly enough that you move around to keep your circulation flowing. Also, taking sleep medications during your flight can cause you to arrive drowsy, making you more of a target for theft or crime.

✿ Staying Healthy on the Road

Water and Food Issues — Microbes are found in all food and water, not just in India. Your body builds up resistance to these little critters in your home country, but when you travel you introduce new microbes into your system. I manage to fare well while on the road, getting sick only when I return from a trip. But I'm very careful about what I consume.

Tap water is unsafe in India. When in a restaurant, always request bottled water. Fruit juices, shakes and ice are quite commonly made from tap water. Restaurants and cafés catering to tourists may be an exception, but it's best to order drinks without ice to be sure.

Drink bottled water (make sure that the cap is sealed prior to opening) or use a portable water purifier, such as the SteriPEN (www.steripen.com). This uses UV light to eradicate parasites, bacteria and protozoa, including giardia. The water won't taste any better, but it will be safe to drink. I've used this on several trips to India and have never had a problem.

Hot Tip! Be sure not to swallow any water while showering, and use bottled or filtered water to brush your teeth.

Small shops specializing in fruits, vegetables, spices and snacks can be found in the cities. These are fun to explore and can be the source of healthful and light snacks. Before purchasing anything, give the shop a good once over to try to determine its overall cleanliness. Check the freshness of anything you purchase by consulting the sell-by date on manufactured products and by eyeballing fruits and vegetables for how fresh they look.

If you're eating in a restaurant that provides silverware, it wouldn't hurt to clean it with a hand wipe and a clean napkin prior to eating.

As the saying goes, cook it, peel it, boil it or forget it. That means no raw veggies or fruits unless they fall into this category. Street food, in contrast, can be quite safe, as it is often cooked right in front of you. If it's been sitting, give it a pass, as flies and mosquitoes may have been buzzing around it for hours.

Eating yogurt or taking a probiotic supplement will help your system stay healthy. Jessica manages to avoid stomach problems by using a probiotic. "Florastor works well and is easy to travel with." Cary takes advantage of the yogurt available in India. "Yogurt introduces local healthy bacteria into the gut and can be very helpful in stabilizing your digestion."

Exercise — If you have an exercise routine at home, stick to it as much as possible. Unless you're staying at a five-star hotel, it's unlikely that your accommodations will have a gym. Instead, you can stretch, practice yoga or do pushups and sit-ups in your room. Few people jog in India, so you're sure to gain lots of attention if you decide to take this up.

When sightseeing, take every opportunity to walk to or around the sights, and try to walk when you are heading out to eat. These small jaunts add up and can really help keep off the pounds and help you to feel fit.

First Aid Kit — While you can purchase a packaged first aid kit, preparing your own is easy. Carry travel-size versions of everything and consolidate pills such as aspirin into well-marked pill cases. I advocate packing light, so carry what is most important for your needs knowing that you can purchase, rather cheaply, anything else upon arrival in India.

Medications

A good generalized kit will include the following:

- sunscreen
- acetaminophen
- anti-diarrheal
- gauze
- blister kit
- pain and fever medication
- antifungal and antibacterial ointments

- antihistamine
- ibuprofen
- cough drops
- tweezers
- antacid

- decongestant
- mild laxative
- bandages
- alcohol wipes
- hydrocortisone cream
- cotton swabs
- tissues

⏣ Female Health Issues

Menstruation — Your period may respond unusually to your travels. You might miss your period completely for months while you're on the road or you may get it when you're least expecting it. This can be caused by stress, heat or as a result of being out of your daily routine. It's nothing to worry about unless it goes on for an unusually extended period of time or if there's a possibility that you're pregnant.

If a problem persists, ask at your nearest embassy or consulate for a recommendation and visit a doctor's office in a city or town with up-to-date testing abilities and equipment. If you suspect you have a serious problem, consider returning home to address the issue.

Contraceptives — If you are on the pill, your period should continue to be regular throughout your travels. Bring enough for the entire trip and note that taking antibiotics can render the pill ineffective.

If there is the slightest possibility that you will be having sex with someone you meet in your travels, carry condoms! And do not be shy about asking your sexual partner to use one. The pill will not give you protection against sexually transmitted diseases — and an STD is the last souvenir you want to bring home.

Yeast Infection — Yeast infections are caused by stress, antibiotics, wearing tight clothing or even wearing a bathing suit for an extended period of time. If you think you have a yeast infection — which is accompanied by itching, discharge, burning during urination, rash and odor — apply an over-the-counter topical vaginal cream and eat yogurt with acidophilus, or see an Ayurvedic or Western-trained doctor for a prescription if symptoms persist for more than a week.

Bladder Infection — Symptoms include burning while urinating, frequent urination and dark-colored urine. A mild case of this will clear up in a few days on its own, but drinking lots of water and/or cranberry juice (which is not readily available in India) will help.

Pregnancy — If you plan to journey to India during a pregnancy, the second trimester is the best time to travel. The worst nausea will be over after the first three months, the risk of a premature delivery will be low in the second trimester, and you may be too uncomfortable to travel during your final months. Airline policies differ, but some outright forbid travel on international flights in the last five weeks of pregnancy.

Bulkhead seats will give you more leg room, but you'll have to place all carry-on bags in the overhead compartment, making it difficult for you to get to your things.

Many vaccinations and medications are either unsafe or untested for pregnant women. If you become infected with a disease such as malaria, it can severely affect your unborn child. Before making travel plans, consult with your doctor in order to avoid potential hazards or problems.

❧ Health Issues You Might Encounter

Sunburn — With the depletion of the ozone layer and the increase in melanomas caused by the sun, you'll want to take extra precautions to avoid getting burned. This is easily preventable by wearing sunscreen and a hat and staying out of the sun. Even short periods of time spent under cloudy skies in the tropics can cause sunburn.

ExOfficio (www.exofficio.com) has a line of clothing, including shirts, hats and handkerchiefs, that utilizes tightly woven fabrics to protect you from the sun's rays.

Delhi Belly — Delhi Belly, or traveler's diarrhea, is quite common amongst travelers to India. This is simply loose bowels caused by bacteria from food or water. It's easily treatable with antibiotics. However, if you aren't on the move and can wait it out, avoid taking antibiotics as these are too often over-prescribed and used improperly. When a full course of antibiotics is not taken, this can cause more virulent strains of bacteria to evolve.

Staying hydrated is extremely important (especially in the heat) and you would do well to take electrolyte supplements to avoid the loss of important nutrients to your body.

Jamie battled Delhi Belly during her travels and learned a little trick from her own experiences. "If you're traveling on your own, be sure to have water on hand at all times so you don't have to leave your room to buy some. When I got sick, I had to be in the bathroom every 20 minutes. I've never had anything run through me so quickly and without water it would have been difficult to get well."

Hot Tip! If you do find yourself ill and unable to leave your room, simply ask the hotel manager or desk clerk to send up some bottled water and/or medication to your room. Since prescriptions are rarely needed in India, acquiring medication should not be an issue.

[handwritten: no need for prescription]

Amoebic Dysentery — The main symptom of amoebic dysentery, caused by contaminated food and water, is bloody diarrhea. Complications of the liver can occur if left untreated. See a doctor immediately if you suspect you've contracted amoebic dysentery.

Motion Sickness — After a big, late meal with friends, we all then drove to their home, a couple of hours away from the restaurant. The roads were terrible and, even though it was late, we were still battling traffic. We swerved, sped ahead, slowed down and moved between cars. By the time we arrived home, I was sick to my stomach. It was nothing more than motion sickness (OK, and too much dahl) but I didn't sleep well all night as a result.

Even paved roads are in poor condition and drivers tend to be unrestrained. Like me, you can easily be affected by the prolonged motion of a long journey under these circumstances.

Quinnette had her own issues with motion sickness but was able to battle it with natural remedies. "I took lozenges that had ginger in them and also ate crystallized ginger. Everyone else in my group got sick but I never had a problem."

Malaria — There are areas of India (including regions below 6,500 feet and in some cities such as Mumbai and Delhi) that will put you at greater risk of contracting malaria. Consult a doctor who specializes in travel medicine to determine the risk factor for the places you'll be visiting. The time of year can also affect your risk.

I haven't taken antimalaria tablets since my first trip to Asia in my early 20s, when I was told to stay out of the sun and that the prescription I was taking was a psychotropic. Since then, I have sought out more natural forms to thwart off mosquitoes and their potential infection.

Nina is very aware of the risks but prefers a more natural approach as well. "Be careful of mosquitoes. You can carry geranium oil in a spray bottle and put it on yourself in the morning or evening when mosquitoes are most active. You can put it on the places where you know you're going to be exposed like your feet or in your socks. It really works."

Hot Tip! Pick up a small bottle of geranium oil in any major Indian city. As one of India's most popular essential oils, you can find it at a pharmacy, Ayurvedic supply store or specialty gift shop.

Plug-in mosquito killers are a popular, and effective, method of ridding your room of mosquitoes. Easily found in pharmacies and grocery stores in India, the liquid-filled bottle gets plugged into a power outlet and releases a vapor that repels and kills mosquitoes. This is one of the first purchases I make upon arrival. The only time I got bitten at night was when I forgot to plug it in.

In addition to their sun-protection products, ExOfficio has a line of clothing that includes a mosquito repellent built into the fabric. I've worn both the pants and blouse throughout India without a mosquito incident. Avoid wearing this clothing for extended periods of time as it is impregnated with chemicals.

Since I am not a medical professional, please check with your doctor or a travel clinic and weigh for yourself the benefits and risks of taking malaria prophylaxis.

Skin Irritations and Problems — Traveling in tropical regions brings its own set of health-related issues and taking proper care of cuts, scratches, bites and skin irritations is paramount. Avoid infections by keeping these covered and avoiding dirty ocean, pool, river or tap water.

If you have mosquito bites, avoid scratching them. Use a soothing oil, cream or gel to calm the irritation. Tea tree oil and cortisone cream are two topicals that have worked well for me.

If you have skin irritations that persist, see a doctor to avoid further infection.

Giardia — Caused by parasites in your gastrointestinal tract, giardia can be really unpleasant, with symptoms that include bloating, severe gas and diarrhea. Avoid dirty water and contaminated food and seek treatment as soon as you suspect that you might have this parasite. It can easily get out of control and multiply.

Hepatitis — If you suspect that you have any form of hepatitis, see a doctor immediately to confirm the diagnosis. There is no treatment for hepatitis A or B. In the case of hep A, you should avoid alcohol and drugs and it should spontaneously resolve itself. For hep B, eat a high-protein/high-carbohydrate diet to repair the potential damage to your liver. Lots of rest will also help.

There is only one treatment for hep C at this time: Intron A, which includes a 24- or 48-week course of medication.

Rabies — Rabies can be fatal if not treated within days of exposure. If you are bitten by an animal that you suspect could be rabid, immediately wash the area with soap, bottled water and an antiseptic iodine solution (if available). You must then see a doctor as soon as possible to start a round of postexposure prophylaxis.

Dengue Fever — Another mosquito-borne illness, this began showing up in India in the 1980s. Symptoms can be more severe than malaria, including high fever, headache and body aches as well as rash and diarrhea. There is no medical treatment or prophylaxis and it can be fatal if the symptoms are not monitored, with the patient getting plenty of rest and hydration. Unlike malaria, dengue is found in urban areas and is transmitted through mosquitoes that feed during the day. Avoid being bitten to ward off the disease.

HIV/AIDS — The virus that causes AIDS is spread through contaminated body fluids. You should never, ever have unprotected sex with an untested partner or come in contact with a needle that has not been sterilized, including those at tattoo parlors and medical facilities. The rate of HIV/AIDS infection in India is growing rapidly.

❧ Managing an Illness on the Road

Doctors and Hospitals — While patients are literally outsourcing their medical care to India now (see Chapter 2, Follow Your Passion, for info on medical treatments), it's not the country where you'd want to end up in the emergency room.

If you do find yourself in need of medical attention, check with your embassy or consulate for referrals to Western-trained doctors and medical facilities that are up to high standards. They can provide you with a list of doctors that are frequently used by the expat community.

Jessica was in a motorbike accident and found herself in the hospital with a broken arm. "I admit the treatment lacked in part but it was also really fascinating to go through their health-care system. You can walk into any hospital and you just pay up front. It cost $3 for an x-ray and $30 for a CAT scan. While the doctor was setting the break, a nurse braided my hair."

Hot Tip! Carry your own syringes in case of an emergency. Also, ask your doctor for a note that gives you permission to carry these in case there are any questions from airport security.

Traditional Medicine — For minor illnesses such as a cold, flu or stomach problems, visit an Ayurvedic doctor. This traditional form of medicine (see Chapter 2, Follow Your Passion, for more information) is practiced by most Indians and is a wonderful alternative to the world of prescription drugs.

Using herbal remedies, vitamins, spices and food combinations, the medicine gets to the root of a problem rather than treating symptoms. While it may take longer for symptoms to disappear, the overall healing process is far more effective.

While I was staying with friends in India, they pulled out a box of bottles that contained various natural remedies, saying, "We never go to the doctor for a prescription. We have everything right here." An excellent book for learning more about Ayurveda, including lists of symptoms and remedies, is *The Complete Book of Ayurvedic Home Remedies* by Vasant Lad.

Hot-oil massages are another important aspect of the Ayurvedic tradition. These amazing massages are given by two individuals who massage your entire body with warm oil as you lie on a slightly convex wooden massage table. At about $10 for an hour, these massages are so cheap there's no excuse not to treat yourself at least once — I had two of these in a week's time in Bangalore. For an additional fee, you can receive a hot-oil drip on your forehead that induces a meditative relaxation.

Safety First

T O *say that India is an unsafe country for women travelers would be an over-statement. However, it's true that foreign women may be targeted by thieves and sexual deviants. Understanding both the socially conservative nature of the country's psyche and the perception of foreign women by Indian men, and then implementing specific safety measures to protect yourself, will go a long way in ensuring safe travels.*

✍ Public Transportation

While at my guesthouse in Udaipur, I met a young gal who had just arrived on an overnight train. Her backpack had been stolen when she left it unattended in order to sleep on a different bunk. She lost everything except her passport and money, which she had slept with.

I noticed several times while traveling in an AC 2-tier sleeper that shortly after boarding, young boys would walk up and down the aisles, presumably taking note of the foreigners and their luggage. I began making a point of immediately locking my bags to my berth with a cable lock so that they would see I was an aware traveler.

Thieves are more opportunistic than violent in India, and there are numerous inexpensive ways to deter potential thieves so that you don't experience the same problem that the young backpacker in Udaipur did.

Always secure your bag(s) to your berth or seat while on public transportation by using a cable lock. If you forget yours from home, you can purchase one at train stations for about 50 cents. These are metal chains with large enough links to fit a lock (not included).

You can also cover your bag with a mesh luggage protector so that it cannot be slit open and the contents emptied. The mesh is wide enough so that this can also be locked to any stationary seat. Pacsafe (www.pacsafe.com) makes these, as well as day bags with slash-proof shoulder straps and panels and other safety features such as tamperproof zippers.

✍ Sexual Harassment

I stopped in at an Internet café in Varanasi. It was a very clean and relatively upscale establishment that offered tourist ser-

TAKING PRECAUTIONS

As a female traveler, it can be quite daunting to hop on a train, bus or metro and have to fend for yourself. Take the following precautions to avoid dangerous situations:

- Travel in ladies-only cars on the train when possible.
- Ride rapid-transit trains during off-peak hours.
- If a man sits next to you on a bus or train and starts getting too close, move to another seat or stand somewhere on the train where you can keep your back (and backside) against the wall of the train as you face any potential gropers
- When traveling in a rickshaw or taxi, keep an arm through the strap of your day bag or attach a small carabiner from your luggage to your belt loop to thwart a thief trying to make a quick grab for your bag.

vices such as cashing travelers checks. The place was empty save for me and one other person using a computer. When the other computer user left, the proprietor introduced himself to me and asked me where I was from. He extended his hand to shake and in doing so, he pulled himself closer to give me a kiss on the cheek. I pushed him away and he apologized, "We do this to greet people." I said, "Not me and not in India."

I'm a hugger at home, but I knew this was not appropriate behavior in India and would have none of it. Fortunately, two Swiss gals I had shared a rickshaw ride with earlier in the day arrived moments after this incident. I immediately told them what happened. Then the power went out (as if the gods were watching out for us) and we left.

If you're a woman traveling without a man at your side, you could very well be the victim of sexual harassment (eve-teasing, as it's called in India), though it doesn't happen to everyone. This can range from sexually explicit comments or catcalls to an outright attack. Eve-teasing is not taken seriously by the authorities. It's usually the victim who is blamed and it often goes unreported by Indian women because of the public shame involved.

Rapes are rare but do occur and have become better publicized in recent years, particularly when a foreigner is involved. Two Japanese girls were gang-raped in Agra after having been slipped a drug in their drinks by three Indian men. Reports of hotel employees attacking solo women travelers have been on the rise. It's unclear whether the number of incidents is truly increasing or if local authorities are now taking these more seriously and they are being reported in the papers more frequently.

Hot Tip! Refuse drinks and food offered by any person unknown to you. Though it may simply be a kind gesture, it's not worth taking your chances.

Nearly as common as henna at a wedding is for a Western woman to be groped, touched or rubbed by men seeking a cheap thrill. Being aware of this potential situation will help ensure that it doesn't go farther than being an annoyance.

Though she's a demure woman, Maliha has spent enough time in India to know how to handle these types of situations. "As American women, we don't want to offend people because we have a PC attitude. We accommodate the culture too much. But it's a traveling hazard of crowded places, and it's naive to think that it won't happen. Don't be silent about it — tell him off like you would in London or New York."

If you know who the culprit is, a stern look and a reprimand-ing shout will completely embarrass him. Often, however, you'll be surrounded by 15 men and you don't know which one is trying to cop a feel. Simply saying, "Stop it" may deter them all from considering how they can get closer to you until you can move to a more protected spot.

While it may not necessarily be eve-teasing, if you're being stared at by a man, don't engage in eye contact — this may may be interpreted as flirtation.

Sumitra, in addition to co-owning Mangosteen, the bed-and-breakfast referral company, runs a tour company in India called Women on Wanderlust (www.wowsumitra.com), and has a lot of worldwide travel experience. As an Indian woman, she has observed just how Western women are perceived by Indian men. "Because of their confidence level, Western women are not intimidated to talk to Indian men, who have a fascination with foreign women. The women will be off their guard and also very vulnerable. Unknowingly, this can cause trouble."

This same self-assurance can work for you. When you're on your own, Pam knows that "confidence is your best compan-ion. Even though you're a tourist, you're less likely to be a tar-get if you travel with confidence."

In short, it's best to appear confident without engaging with men one on one.

Jamie was walking around Nainital with her friend. "A man stopped us and said, 'Hello. Where's your hotel? Or do you want to go to my hotel?' We just told him to get lost."

She didn't let this bother her too much. "There is a stereotype of loose Western women, that they will sleep with anyone. Perhaps this guy was trying his luck to see if the stereotype was true. We never felt threatened but neither did we feel comfortable walking down an alley where there were few people except for a couple of men."

↬ Police

The police are notoriously disinterested in helping anyone. If you do get into a pickle, you may have a hard time finding help, but don't let that dissuade you from asking. For any sort of crime — from passport theft to rape — report the issue immediately to the local authorities and request a written report so that the issue goes on record. Alert your local embassy or consulate as well. Depending on the crime, they may be able to help you.

If your personal belongings are stolen, there's little chance they will be recovered. You'll still need to file a report, however, to receive reimbursement from your credit card or insurance company.

Tourism Police — A taxi driver tried to extract double the agreed-upon amount from me and my friend when he dropped us off at the airport. He insisted that it was his company's policy to charge more for two people even though he previously quoted us a fare based on our sharing the ride. After some back and forth, I simply suggested that we go find the tourist police to settle the situation. He quickly backed off. We grabbed our bags, paid him the original fare quoted and headed inside. There was no argument.

I didn't even know if there were tourism police officers in the area, but it was an effective threat.

The role of the tourism police is to protect tourists, help them avoid harassment by touts and provide a resource against cheats like my taxi driver. Some cities have a squad of jeeps that patrol the streets in order to manage complaints by tourists. In addition, tourism police can be found in designated booths set up in railway stations, airports and major tourist sites.

How much help they will be really depends, but simply using this as a threat may be helpful, as it shows you have some degree of knowledge about India.

↝ Drugs

Don't be fooled into thinking that the ready availability of drugs such as marijuana, hashish, cocaine, acid and ecstasy make them legal in India. They are not.

They are quite prevalent in the party-havens of Goa and other beach resorts that attract hordes of young backpackers. In small villages and even in cities, their presence is not obvious unless you're looking for them.

Marijuana use is tolerated to a certain degree by authorities. Police tend to turn a blind eye and you may find the weed listed on menus as part of a drink or baked into some goodies — think: Happy Meal.

Because many of these drugs are widely available, you may be lulled into a false sense of security that it is alright to participate in their use. Don't believe that you are above the law and that you can easily get out of a drug-related arrest. Not all police can be bought off with a few rupees, and getting busted could land you in jail.

Stories have circulated for years about drugs being planted in tourists' rooms by the police in an effort to extract baksheesh from the hapless hippies. During my time in Goa many years ago, I would place a piece of tape over my hotel room door or put a slip of paper in the crack so that I could tell if anyone had been in my room. No one ever foiled my clever little seal, but at least I had some peace of mind that I could call the hotel manager immediately if I suspected foul play.

Hot Tip! Steer clear of any activity that could land you in jail. Though you may be tempted to indulge while you're away from home, the consequences are not worth it.

⚭ Passport

If your passport is lost or stolen while in India, immediately contact the local authorities so that you have documentation of the loss. Also report this to your embassy or consulate, which will need a copy of the police report in order to issue a replacement. See Chapter 5, The Practicalities, for more information on passports.

Keep a photocopy of your passport either on your person, in your hotel room, at home (where a friend can access it) or as a scanned copy that you've emailed yourself. Having a copy of your passport handy will make the replacement process easier.

You can have your passport replaced at an embassy in Mumbai or Delhi. You can also get a temporary passport in Chennai, Kolkata or Panjim.

⚭ Keeping Money Safe

Carrying travelers checks and debit or credit cards is the easiest way to ensure that you don't lose hard cash. Contact your bank immediately upon learning you've lost your card(s) to minimize potential charges to your account. Credit card companies provide more protection in these situations than banks issuing debit cards. As long as you have a copy of your travelers check numbers, you can be reimbursed for these.

Always carry the direct phone number for your bank(s) to report any issues. Toll-free numbers do not work when calling from India, but your bank will accept collect calls.

See Chapter 5, The Practicalities, for more information on carrying cash.

❧ Hotels

There was a rash of attacks on foreign women by hotel staff in early 2007. This occurred from Goa to Kerala to Agra. To deter an assault, rape or molestation, avoid conversation with male hotel staff, dress conservatively and never let a male in your room, even someone from room service or a repair person. Your friendliness can easily be misconstrued.

It's not unheard-of to have someone (usually an employee) enter your hotel room while you're out sightseeing or even while you're in the room showering or sleeping. To prevent someone from getting into your room while you're inside, place a rubber door stop, easily purchased at a hardware store at home, under your hotel room door. Most hotel room doors open inwards and quite often don't have a chain or bolt in addition to the handle lock. The rubber door stop will prevent the door from opening.

Many hotel rooms, particularly those at budget and mid-range accommodations, are locked with a padlock provided by the hotel. Though most places are trustworthy, why take chances? The best way to prevent theft is to carry your own padlock or combination lock to use on the door. This may not make it impossible for someone to break in, but it will discourage a key-happy employee from trying.

If I'm not able to lock a room with my own padlock, when I leave for the day I lock my luggage zippers together with a tiny lock and then use a cable lock to secure the entire bag to a piece of furniture in the room.

Hot Tip! If you're staying in a dorm-style guesthouse, it's best to request a room with a private bath so you don't have to roam the halls where the (male) hotel staff can watch your comings and goings.

When traveling solo, I carry a keychain-style high-decibel alarm and sleep with it next to my bed. Though I've never had to use it, if an intruder were to enter my room I would enable the alarm so as to scare him off and alert others.

I have never used a hotel's safe located behind the reception desk. I will, however, use a safe if it's in the room and I am unable to use my own padlock on the door.

PACK IT UP

W e hip chicks don t want to be caught without our favorite travel shoes and capris. But the reality is that packing light is the key to making your travels comfortable and safe. It allows you to easily maneuver through airports and bus and train stations, and avoid spending hours packing and unpacking in your hotel room. Use the suggestions in this chapter to pack only what you need and weed out the excess clothing and accessories that may get little use on the road.

∾ Conservative Clothing

Even if the purpose of your trip is to relax on the beaches of Goa or Pondicherry, as a woman, you'll still want to carry some clothing that is conservative in nature.

Dressing appropriately sets the tone of how you are received by the locals (and potentially other travelers) and will help ensure that unwanted attention and advances from men are kept to a minimum. Low-cut and/or tight-fitting shirts, skirts that fall above the knees, shorts and bikinis are highly discouraged. While swimsuits can be worn at the beach or in the privacy of your hotel's pool area, consider a conservative one-piece rather than a bikini. Cover yourself with a sarong and T-shirt when not sunbathing or when you are interacting with locals.

If you're traveling in warmer climates and cities frequented by tourists, short-sleeve cotton shirts are OK, but they should be loose fitting and not revealing. Observe the locals and dress a bit more conservatively than the most liberally dressed Indian woman.

Cotton pants and a light short-sleeve shirt are appropriate in beach towns and in major cities where the locals are used to seeing tourists in more revealing clothes. Jeans and a long-sleeve shirt or sweater are perfect for colder climates and in rural areas where you'll gain more respect with conservative attire.

While Bollywood beauties are seen in advertisements and movies wearing provocative clothing, the same low-cut or see-through-style blouses are off-limits to the rest of the population, and this means travelers, too.

Denise had a conversation with a well-educated Indian woman during a long bus ride. "It was so hot when we were there that my friend and I were wearing tank tops but with long pants. This woman said that the men thought we were prostitutes because we were baring our shoulders."

↬ Purchase Clothes When You Arrive

FabIndia is the store for me! With outlets throughout the country, it's a great place to shop both when I arrive in India (to purchase clothes for my trip) and at the end of my trip (to purchase clothes to take home).

Hot Tip! When buying clothes at a store that doesn't have fixed prices, always bargain before you try it on. You've lost some of your bargaining power if the shopkeeper knows how much you like the item.

It's easy to incorporate some of the local dress into your outfits and India is a super-easy country in which to purchase clothes once you arrive. Clothes will be cheap and adopting the styles will help you fit in.

I recommend bringing only the clothes on your back and perhaps packing one blouse to change into on your first full day. Make that first day a shopping day and purchase an extra top or two and a pair of Western pants or loose-fitting *salwar* (the pants of a *salwar kameez*).

For bigger gals this may be a bit more difficult, but tailors can use local materials to fashion an Indian outfit or copy a style you already own. No matter your size, your purchase can be as simple as a locally made blouse or a delicate *dupatta* (scarf) worn over your Western-style clothes. The *dupatta* will also come in handy when you need to cover up your arms or head.

Larger cities have department stores where Western fashions are available but are made with Indian materials and prints.

These can be a bit pricey (still only two-thirds the price you'd pay in North America), but you're sure to find some interesting outfits that you'd never get back home.

Saris and Salwar Kameez — A *salwar kameez* is a comfortable outfit that is worn by every Indian woman. The kameez itself is a loose-fitting blouse, either with three-quarter or full-length sleeves, that comes down past the waist or just above the knees. The salwar is a loose-fitting pajama-like pant that is very wide at the top and very narrow at the ankle. You can purchase these at department stores and small boutiques, or have them tailor-made (recommended if you are a larger size) for a very reasonable price.

Laura took advantage of the low cost of handmade clothes during her journey. "I bought three cotton *salwar kameez* outfits from simple storefronts in Bangalore. Custom alterations are part of the purchase! I wore those a lot. They were perfect for hot weather and made me feel more anonymous in a crowd. I also bought a couple of saris so that I could blend in more, but I only wore one on the street once. A Western woman in a sari does not pass unnoticed. Random people were coming up to me and telling me how beautiful I was. My plan was foiled because I got so much attention."

Saris are worn by all Indian women at one time or another, but are rarely worn by Western women except, perhaps, for a special occasion such as a wedding. It consists of a long length of fabric wrapped elegantly, and without pins, zippers or buttons, around the body and over a *choli* (a short-sleeve and often midriff-baring top). While a *choli* may seem revealing to the Western eye because the stomach often shows, it should never be worn alone without a sari or other fabric covering it up. This would be akin to wearing just your bra outside your home.

In her sari, Margie felt like she blended in more but she still got some attention. "When I would wear a sari, the men would say 'very nice Indian dress. Thank you for wearing our dress.'"

Jessica kept her dress style simple yet in keeping with the locals. She found that this helped connect her with the culture. "I have a nose ring and I wore a *bindi* [forehead decoration]. You can't underestimate the importance of wearing the local clothes."

Indian women take great pride in their beauty and take special care in choosing their attire. A gentleman who had just sold me more than a hundred dollars worth of silver jewelry in Jaipur suggested that I wear something more Indian so that, even after two and a half weeks of travel, I didn't look like I just got off the plane. After that, I felt boyish and self-conscious in my generic T-shirt and light jacket — until I added a beautiful silk scarf to my outfit!

❧ Toiletries

Feminine Products — While they can be found in larger cities, tampons and pads are not as readily available in India as they are in the West. I personally recommend using the DivaCup (www.divacup.com) or something similar. Made of a soft medical-grade silicone, the DivaCup collects menstrual flow and, depending on your cycle, only needs to be emptied once or twice every 24 hours. This eco-friendly product is safe and easy to use, and I never travel without it. Because they are not quite as clean as inserting a tampon, carry hand wipes to wash up.

Alternately, carry enough OB tampons (which pack easily) for the duration of your trip or, if you're traveling for an extended length of time, be on the lookout for feminine products and purchase them when you find them so you don't get caught short.

Toilet Paper — While it's readily available in shops, toilet paper is rarely provided in public toilets, including on domestic flights. Though you may want to pack one for the road, it's easy enough to purchase rolls once you arrive. Always carry at least a few squares with you at all times or get used to using your left hand.

Hot Tip! Buy a "to go" roll of toilet paper from the travel section of your local pharmacy. These are made without the cardboard tube so they are super small and easy to carry.

Shampoos, Conditioners and Lotions — The latest carry-on rules from the Transportation Security Administration (www.tsa.gov) prohibit you from carrying large bottles of liquids and gels (including shampoos, conditioners, lotions, hairspray, gels, etc.) in your carry-on bag. Three ounces is the maximum per bottle and all of these liquids and gels must fit into a quart-size zip-top bag.

During a one-month trip to India, in which I didn't check any bags, I only carried three-ounce bottles of both shampoo and conditioner and even had shampoo left over (though I admit to not washing my hair daily).

I also carried body lotion, hair gel and a facial cleanser in smaller bottles and fit these all in a small sandwich bag. I did run out of lotion but purchased more while in India.

Hot Tip! After years of packing a travel-sized toothbrush and never quite feeling satisfied with its performance, I finally started carrying my favorite toothbrush. Now my teeth always feel clean and my mouth fresh.

✢ Accessories

Earplugs — Though earplugs can be slightly uncomfortable to wear, they're far better than listening to the 5 a.m. call to prayer after your middle-of-the-night arrival. They take up so little space that there's no reason not to tuck a few pairs in your toiletry bag. Pam never leaves home without them. "I always take earplugs. They are essential for trains and noisy hotels."

Keep a few sets of earplugs handy for loud guesthouses, long flights, overnight train rides with chatty locals and bus rides. Test out several kinds before your departure so that you find some that fit well and filter out enough noise to keep you snoozing happily.

Eyeshades — I don't travel anywhere without my eyeshade. It comes in quite handy for long flights, overnight train rides and in hotels where a street lamp is shining through sheer curtains. It's also super light and easy to tuck into a day bag.

Hot Tip! Buy rubber flip-flops when you arrive. You'll love having a pair of slip-on shoes to wear in the shower and to the toilet on overnight train trips. They'll set you back no more than $2.

11. PACK IT UP

✢ Technology

Power Adapter — In order to use your electronic equipment in India, you'll need an adapter that will convert your two- or three-pronged North American plug into the plug with two round pegs required on the subcontinent (as well as other Asian countries). These can be found at any travel goods store or website.

Hot Tip! Many power outlets have a switch that turns the power on and off. If your electronics don't seem to be working, check to make sure the outlet is actually switched on.

Digital Camera — Digital cameras have become de rigueur for travelers. Gone are the hordes of film canisters, the storage issues and the cost of developing that accompany shooting film.

Though digital photography is far easier with regards to the amount of equipment and number of accessories involved, there are some things that are particular to this sort of shooting.

You'll need to pack a docking station or battery charger if your camera has an internal battery. Carry plenty of memory cards made from a reputable manufacturer and back up your digital images often.

Hot Tip! If you fall short on GB, you can purchase memory cards in India's larger cities. Buy a reputable brand and test it out before you leave the shop. I lost 10 days' worth of photos (including Varanasi!) because the Indian-made memory card I purchased had gone bad.

Cary travels to India frequently, spending months at a time there and taking lots of digital images. "I back them up on CDs that any Internet café can burn. I carry a little USB device and insert my memory card to transfer them to the computer, but every Internet café has card readers. I also back up images on my iPod, which functions as a hard drive."

If you're not keen on using your iPod for photo storage and you don't want to be tied to an Internet café, try the Digital Foci (www.digitalfoci.com) Photo Safe portable hard drive for images. It's available with up to 120 GB of storage.

Film Camera — If you are shooting film, you are probably particular about the type of film you use. Carry more than you expect to shoot, as film availability in India will be limited. If you will be in extreme heat or cold, protect the film with an insulated bag and keep it out of direct sunlight. While you might want to have a roll or two developed along the way to ensure your camera is working properly, consider waiting until you're home, where the processing is more reliable, to develop the bulk of your film.

Do not allow your film to go through x-ray machines, either on your international flight or on any domestic flights. Politely ask security to hand check it.

Mp3 Player — I always did enjoy traveling with a tape player or Discman during my early days of travel. Now, I carry my iPod, which serves several purposes. Not only does it play back the thousands of songs I have uploaded but it also has an external microphone attachment (called the iTalk) with which I can easily record sounds, music, interviews and conversations. I love playing these back months after I've returned from India. It immediately conjures up the experiences that went along with a given place.

Courtney used her mp3 player for another use. "I brought an iPod and mini speakers so that when I was in a hotel room I could listen to music and feel more at home. Having the speakers was also really social. When I got together with people, it made it really nice."

Audiobooks — I may not be hooked on phonics, but I am hooked on audiobooks. With a novel or memoir that takes place in India or elsewhere, I feel like I have an extra friend traveling with me as I listen to the lulling sound of the reader's voice whether I'm drifting off to sleep or taking a long train ride. These can easily be downloaded from iTunes (www. itunes.com), Amazon (www.amazon.com) and other online resources.

Ebook Readers — Amazon and Sony (www.sonystyle.com) both manufacture ebook (electronic book) readers, devices onto which you can download full-length books and read them on-screen. Slightly smaller, and much thinner, than a paperback book, Amazon's Kindle can hold up to 200 books, and Sony's Reader Digital Book holds up to 160 books.

The units are pricey, at $400 for the Kindle and $300 for the Reader Digital Book. The downloadable books have to be purchased separately but are cheaper than the paper version. The Kindle comes with a power adapter as well as a USB cable. Unless you're traveling with your laptop and can use the USB cable as a power source, you'll need to purchase the power adapter for the Reader Digital Book as it's sold separately.

Laptop — I often get asked if I carry my laptop when I travel. "Never outside of the U.S." is my answer. Instead, I do my writing the old-fashioned way — with a fresh, fabulous travel journal and a new pen. A laptop is too precious a piece of equipment for me to risk taking it on the road. I feel that the potential for theft and breakage is just too high.

However, you may need your laptop for business or you may simply feel more comfortable carrying one than I do. Wireless availability is just starting to pop up in India and you may have luck finding it in a café or at your hotel. Keep in mind that it will be difficult to find a spare power cord if you've lost yours, or a repair shop if your laptop needs servicing.

Noise-Canceling Headphones — These bulky battery-powered headphones do an amazing job at cutting out background noise. There's no comparison between these and earbuds that slip right into your ears. The noise-canceling headphones can be plugged into your own mp3 device or into the jack in your airplane seat so that you can listen to the in-flight entertainment.

Because of their ungainliness, I've never tried sleeping with them on and have only used them to watch in-flight movies. Honestly? It's a toss-up as to whether these might be worth packing into your carry-on bag all the way to India, as you may have no other use for them except on the flight. They're pricey, too, at about $300 for a pair of Bose (www.bose.com).

⌁ Types of Packs and Luggage

Garment Bag — If you're traveling to India for business, a garment bag is your best option for packing dress clothes. Bags are available as bi- or tri-folds and some can even fold up small enough to slip under the airplane seat in front of you.

Pack as little as possible so that you aren't hauling around a bag with heavy slacks and suit jackets.

Choose a bag with a variety of pockets located outside and inside and utilize these for your underwear and other smaller items. Wear your heaviest shoes and pack additional ones away. You're probably carrying your most expensive outfits, so purchase a high-quality bag that won't easily rip or tear.

While you may not be able to eliminate all creases and wrinkles, using plastic dry cleaning bags between each layer of clothing can help cut down on these when the bag is folded and stored on the plane.

Backpack / Roll-Aboard Combinations — During a month-long trip, I carried a combination backpack/roll-aboard bag that was, at 22", small enough to use as a carry-on. It quickly converted to a backpack for those times when I was walking along dirt roads and back to a roll-aboard when I arrived at the airport.

Whether you're a "backpacker" or simply a casual traveler, these small convertible carry-ons can, even for extended travel, accommodate all you'll need for your trip.

The shoulder straps adjust to suit your body size. These combination packs often come with daypacks that zip off and they open up like a suitcase for easy packing. Some are even made to specifically fit a woman's body type.

A travel backpack will work well also. These include most of the same features as the combination pack, lacking only the wheels. With their suitcase-like opening, many include additional interior pockets, straps to hold items in place and outer pockets for water bottles and other items you may want to access quickly, as well as a zip-off day bag.

Wilderness Packs — For trekkers, wilderness packs are more comfortable than combination backpacks because they balance better on your back. They are top loading, making them a little harder to pack and unpack, and they rarely come with day bags attached.

Hot Tip! Keep your bags safe by using a TSA-approved lock. By using one of these to lock your zippers together, you can prevent the contents from spilling out as well as stop a casual thief from opening the bag and sorting through the contents. The TSA-approved locks can be opened by airport security people using specially designed tools.

Day Bags — The right day bag is indispensable. It needs to be small enough to slip under the airplane seat in front of you, yet large enough to carry everything you need for a day out. A bag that is worn across your body, such as a shoulder bag or messenger bag, is more desirable than a purse or small backpack. Pacsafe manufactures a variety of day bags that are slash-proof and can be worn as a shoulder bag or hip pack. There's plenty of space for your guidebook, water, camera and journal.

❧ Creature Comforts

If this is your first trip to India, you are probably going to be out of your comfort zone. Way out. To help offset some of the discomfort of swimming in a sea of unknown food, languages, smells and sights, it's always good to have some of your favorite (little) items from home.

I met a woman on the banks of the Ganges who was watching over the burning ghats in the early-morning hours with a thermos of coffee. I asked her if she was living in Varanasi and nodded my head at her thermos. "No, I just like my creature comforts," was her response.

When we're plunked down in the middle of strange lands, something as simple as a cup of coffee can help us cope with the culture shock that we will surely experience at one point or another.

It doesn't have to be your favorite coffee thermos. Perhaps it's an amulet from your niece that you wear around your neck, a good luck coin you keep in your pocket or your favorite chocolate bar that you unwrap when you feel as though everything else is unraveling around you.

Pam carries rosemary oil. "I use it to clear my sinuses on the plane and when I'm in a less than luxurious hotel with a mildew problem. I put a drop on my nose and it stimulates my sinuses so they don't dry out."

Your creature comfort might also be your hobby. Perhaps you enjoy knitting or crossword puzzles. These could also be conversation starters with the local women.

Hot Tip! Don't carry anything of real or sentimental value, such as expensive jewelry, with you to India. Your only valuables should include your passport, cash, travelers checks, credit and debit cards and any electronic equipment, all of which can be easily replaced.

❧ Gifts

Traveling companions and locals alike will be appreciative of small inexpensive gifts. When traveling to developing countries, I shop at my local dollar store in Seattle to pile up on items to share, including key chains featuring the Space Needle or Mount Rainier, and beaded bracelets, candy, wind-up toys and pencils for children.

Sigrid brought stickers with her to India. Rather than giving money to begging children, she handed out these. "I gave them to kids so they would have something. I also brought unused toothbrushes that I had picked up at hotels and would give those to the kids."

When invited into someone's home as either an overnight guest or for a meal, I give nicer items from the Pacific Northwest including locally made chocolates, small bags of ground coffee or vacuum-packed salmon.

Hot Tip! Carry postcards from your home city. These help to break down barriers and start conversations with taxi drivers and ice cream vendors alike.

Though I never check luggage on my way to India, I always buy an extra bag at the end of my trip to carry home the souvenirs I've purchased for myself and others. This I do have to check.

❧ Packing Lists

Limiting the amount of clothes you bring and purchasing additional items once you arrive means you'll only need one carry-on bag for your tip (in addition to a day bag). Wear your heaviest items on the plane and dress in layers so that your bag is light enough for you to lift it into the overhead bin.

I pack my few wearables into a compression sack that squeezes the air out of them and into about 1/3 their size. I put my electronics and their power cords and docking stations into a padded packing cube and then include my toiletries (that don't have to be hand-scanned by security) in their own case. I top it all off with one spare pair of sandals and a book or two.

Here's what I typically bring with me for a one-month trip to the subcontinent:

Clothes

- Jeans *
- Light jacket *
- Underwear *
- Pajamas
- Teva sandals for daily walking
- Short-sleeve blouse *
- Sandals with light socks *
- Convertible pants/shorts
- Bathing suit
- Light sweater *
- Bras *
- Long-sleeve shirt
- Belt

Toiletries

- Shampoo **
- Toothpaste **
- Dental floss
- Vitamins
- Hair ties
- Tissues
- Conditioner **
- Hand lotion **
- Toothbrush
- Medications
- DivaCup
- Razor
- Deodorant **
- Facial lotion **
- Lip balm
- Hairbrush
- Makeup

Accessories and Documents

- Passport (with visa)
- Credit/debit cards
- Cash
- Journal and pens
- Eyeshade
- Insurance information
- Books/guidebooks
- Electricity converter
- iPod (and charger)
- Flashlight (and batteries)
- Sleep sack
- Day bag

- Flight confirmation and/or boarding pass
- Travelers checks
- Phrase book
- Emergency contact info
- Sunglasses
- Magazines
- Camera (and charger)
- Video camera (and charger)
- Cell phone (and charger)
- Snacks
- Business cards
- Money belt

---

* What I wear on the plane. I bring two pairs of ExOfficio under-wear, packing one pair and wearing the other.

** These must go in 3 oz. or less containers, fit into a sandwich-size plastic bag and be hand-checked by security.

RESPONSIBLE TRAVEL

INDIA'S *infrastructure is not quite ready for prime time when it comes to eco-friendly and responsible tourism or even recycling. Any Wanderluster with the slightest tinge of green will be dismayed when she sees the number of water bottles, empty cookie wrappers, cardboard boxes and terra-cotta chai cups that litter sidewalks, streets and alleys. Don't let seeing this trash turn you into a uncaring litterbug yourself. Rise to the occasion and be aware of how you can be part of the solution.*

My friend Helen used to say that people in the developing world were the greatest recyclers because they would pick up plastic and glass bottles, cans and discarded materials to reuse and recycle. While Indians can be crafty — welding together broken rickshaw parts because they can't afford new ones; reusing bottles, bags and even straws; and patching up furniture and other household items till the bitter end of their usefulness — there is no sense of "recycling" as we know it in the West.

While our individual impact as travelers on an already overburdened environment may seem insignificant, and India's issues insurmountable, it is the responsibility of every traveler to understand just what we can do to lessen our impact on India and the world in general.

As Jessica notes, "India isn't the easiest place in the world to engage in environmentally responsible travel. There's so much trash in the streets that you can see cows eating plastic bags." Given the reverence cows receive, this seems quite ironic, but it is endemic to India's immense garbage problem.

According to Shivala, the woman I met on my overnight train ride, "There was a time when farmers would relieve themselves in the fields, helping to fertilize the soil." They "progressed" to using outhouses and dumping chemicals on their fields. Shivala continued, "They now throw trash and other nonbiodegradable materials into the soil rather than leaves and compostables, which were once used."

While the West's influence has provided some beneficial results to the country's development, it has obviously not all been positive. Conversely, not all issues should be blamed on the West. Pollution, overpopulation and deforestation are also factors in India's environmental degradation.

In some areas, the local population is beginning to understand the impact of development as they experience water shortages and declining nutrients in the soil due to the overuse of pesticides. In the state of Bihar, for example, farmers are now reducing the amount of pesticides used in order to re-introduce nutrients back into the soil. Throughout India, organic farming is becoming more popular.

How can you as an individual possibly make a difference? Well, there are many ways for you to tread lightly during your journey.

⮞ Transportation

The public transportation system in India isn't half bad. Buses, trains and rapid transit connect within and among cities. Auto- and cycle-rickshaws can then easily get you to your specific destination. To help cut down on emissions, public transportation in Delhi and Ahmedabad is required to run on compressed natural gas (CNG). It's a good start, but all cities in India still have tremendous pollution problems. Do your part to make sure they don't get any worse.

While hiring a taxi for a full day of sightseeing can be incredibly cheap, planning out your day and taking a bus or train to your destination is far gentler on the environment. If you do hire a private driver, asking for a car rather than an SUV can also make a difference (and will be cheaper).

Hot Tip! When traveling short distances within a city, choose to walk rather than take a taxi or auto-rickshaw. This will help you stay in shape and reduce carbon emissions.

12. RESPONSIBLE TRAVEL

ECO-FRIENDLY TRANSPORTATION

When considering how to get to your destination, consider these options, from most to least environmentally friendly:

In city:

1. walk
2. cycle-rickshaw
3. bus
4. rapid transit/metro
5. auto-rickshaw
6. taxi

Between cities:

1. train
2. bus
3. shared shuttle/SUV (these run in the Himalayas where there are no trains)
4. private car and driver (for longer distances)
5. airplane

↝ Trash

Hopefully you'll be so enamored with the vast choices (and low cost) of fresh food available that you'll resist the temptation to gorge on packaged, processed foods from a grocery store. While I fully trust that you would not toss your empty packaging on the streets, why even contribute to the ultimate problem at all? Stick with whole foods (and organic ones, when possible) that don't require a wrapper!

It's really no surprise that Indians so flippantly toss their garbage on the streets since it is difficult to find trash containers anywhere. Knowing this, you can at least be prepared by carrying a paper bag designated for your own trash. Dump it when you do find a receptacle or when you return to your hotel.

As Jessica mentioned, cows, so sacred to Hindus, eat from piles of garbage and die from ingesting the plastic bags since their systems cannot process them. Fortunately, some cities and villages are banning the manufacture and use of plastic bags. After severe flooding in Mumbai in 2005, the government of Maharashtra State began to implement a ban, as it was believed the plastics drastically contributed to clogged drainage systems, worsening the water damage.

Hot Tip! When you make a purchase, just say no — to a plastic bag, that is. Instead, use your day bag for any items you pick up along the way, or consolidate your purchases into one large shopping bag.

Purchasing electronics with rechargeable batteries also cuts down on the amount of waste that you generate. Angela, who is an eco-travel blogger at Wanderlust and Lipstick (www. wanderlustandlipstick.com), explains the issue with regards to batteries. "Disposable batteries are especially noxious as they leach toxic chemicals into the earth." If your electronics don't have a built-in charger, she suggests that "the more responsible (and, conveniently, more economical) option is to bring a charger and rechargeable batteries."

↝ Water

Delhi's groundwater situation is dire. The city does not have enough for its residents, who use more water per capita on a daily basis than anywhere else in the country. Nearly half the population does not have access to piped water, and the quality of that water is questionable. Since Delhi is a city that relies on hydroelectric power, it's easy to understand why there are so many power outages.

Neither you nor I will solve Delhi's water shortage issue, but being an aware consumer of this precious commodity can't hurt.

Did you know that it takes 250 liters of water to make the sugar for one liter of Coca-Cola? Drink water, and when you drink water, make it tap. Yes, even in India, you can drink the tap water if it's properly purified.

Cary steers away from bottled water whenever possible. "To cut down on plastic bottle use, I use an ultraviolet purifier for tap water called the SteriPEN. I also use a thermos and always fill it with boiled water from a restaurant or guesthouse. I then let it cool down and put it into a clean plastic bottle for out-and-about use."

Beyond what you choose to imbibe, you can cut down on your water impact by taking short showers and not allowing the water to run in the sink while washing up. Though they may exist, I've never stayed in a hotel in India that offered "green cleaning," in which you have the option to reuse your towels by placing them on a towel rack rather than on the floor (which indicates you'd like them washed). If there is a daily cleaning service, I simply leave the "Do Not Disturb" sign on the doorknob and my room goes undisturbed, including my towels, which I'm happy to reuse.

✺ Carbon Offsetting

You may choose to utilize a carbon buy-back program to lessen the impact of your travels to India. Programs such as

TerraPass (www.terrapass.com) calculate the amount of carbon dioxide you're generating and offer ways in which you can offset these through financial contributions. These contributions are then channeled into programs that reduce carbon emissions, such as wind farms.

A flight from Seattle to Delhi, incidentally, produces nearly 6,000 pounds of carbon dioxide per individual. Yikes. Fortunately, the offset cost for this is under $30.

12. RESPONSIBLE TRAVEL

13.

COMING HOME

R eturning home after a journey to India
may not be easy. Though being immersed
in a foreign culture may have you longing
for familiarity, the reentry into your own environment may be difficult.

When I return home from a trip to the subcontinent, in addition to fending off jet lag, I find myself in the throes of reverse culture shock, in which my own city and neighborhood are foreign to me. Seattle appears sterile, quiet and closed-in. Where are the people? The traffic? The cows? And why is everything so expensive?

Back home, my first visit to the grocery store is always jarring. Walking down the aisles, I find the variety of soda and chips at my disposal to be disturbing. It's no wonder the Western world has an obesity epidemic – we truly have too many choices. This is in stark contrast to the world of India, where the vast majority have few options available not only with regards to food, but jobs and housing as well.

I feel truly blessed to not only have access to all of these options but to have access to the world beyond my own borders. Though there is debate that staying close to home, as opposed to traveling, is better for the environment, I believe that leaving your community and country to visit other regions brings peace and stability into the world. And, while the environment *is* important, so is loving and understanding your fellow man (and woman).

My wish is that this guide will help you to better appreciate India so that you may slip into her world with patience, tolerance and acceptance. And then, slip back into your own world with this same approach.

Namaste,

Beth

GLOSSARY

bang lassi — yogurt drink laced with marijuana

bhojanalaya — local restaurant often found at truck stops

bindi — forehead decoration worn by Indian women

chapatti — unleavened cooked flat bread

chang — alcoholic drink most often home made by Tibetans

choli — short sleeved and often midriff-baring top

dahl — beans

dhaba — local restaurant often found at truck stops

dharmashala — place of worship at a Jain, Buddhist, or Muslim
temple

Diwali — festival of lights

dosa — south India crepe

doshas — the body types as defined in Ayurvedic medicine

dowry — money or goods given to a husband and his family by the
bride

dupatta — long scarf

ghat — broad steps leading to a river

ghee — clarified butter

gurudwaras — place of worship for Sikhs

Holi — festival of color

idli — rice and lentil savory cake eaten for breakfast or as a snack

jalebi — fried batter dipped in syrup

kapha — one of the three dosha types found in Ayurvedic medicine

khadi — hand-woven cloth

Kumbh Mela — Hindu pilgrimage

humanitour — a trip that includes volunteer work

lassi — blended yogurt and water drink

naan — round flat bread made of flour and water

namaste — common greeting, meaning "I recognize the spirit in you."

paneer — cubed cheese

pani puri — round, hollow fried crisp

paratha — flatbread often filled with vegetables

puja — religious ritual or prayer that shows respect to a god or gods

raga — melodic modes in Indian music

raita — yogurt or relish dish made with spices, herbs, and vegetables

salwar kameez — traditional dress consisting of blouse and pants

sambar — literally a dish incorporating many spices but can also be
found as a spice only

Sankrathi — harvest festival celebrated throughout the country

sari — traditional dress made of one long piece of cloth

sitar — plucked string instrument used in Hindustani classical music

tabla — percussion instruments played with the hands

taddy — alcoholic drink made in West Bengal

tatkal — a ticket provided by Indian railways used by last-minute
travelers

thali — a selection of different dishes served together on one plate

thandai — a cashew milk drink consumed during Holi

tumba — alcoholic drink most often home made by Tibetans

vata — one of three dosha types in Ayurvedic medicine

wallah — person who performs a specifc duty as selling items from a
street cart

WEBSITE RESOURCES

Akhand Pratap Singh, palm reader — www.bestpalmreader.com
Amazon — www.amazon.com
Bike Friday — www.bikefriday.com
Blogger — www.blogger.com
Board of Control for Cricket in India — www.bcci.cricket.deepthi.com
Bose — www.bose.com
Central Board of Film Certification — www.cbfcindia.tn.nic.in
Cleartrip — www.cleartrip.com
Cocoon — www.cocoonusa.com
Couchsurfing — www.couchsurfing.com
Craigslist — http://geo.craigslist.org/iso/in
Crate Works — www.crateworks.com
Cricinfo — www.cricinfo.com
Digital Foci — www.digitalfoci.com
DivaCup — www.divacup.com
ExOfficio — www.exofficio.com
Expedia — www.expedia.com
Explore Rural India — www.exploreruralindia.org
Facebook — www.facebook.com
Fodor's Travel Talk — www.fodors.com/forums
Ginkgo Press — www.ginkgopress.com
Global Freeloaders — www.globalfreeloaders.com
Google Groups — http://groups.google.com
Guild of Service — www.guildofserviceni.com
Home Exchange — www.homeexchange.com
Hospitality Club — www.hospitalityclub.org
Hostelling International — www.hihostels.com
India Mike — www.indiamike.com
Incredible India — www.incredibleindia.org
Indian Cricket League — www.indiancricketleague.in

Indian Railways — **www.indianrail.gov.in**

InsureMyTrip.com — **www.insuremytrip.com**

iTunes — **www.itunes.com**

Jet Airways — **www.jetairways.com**

Kingfisher Airlines — **www.flykingfisher.com**

Lonely Planet — **www.lonelyplanet.com**

Lonely Planet Thorn Tree Travel Forum —
   www.lonelyplanet.com/thorntree

Make My Trip — **www.makemytrip.com**

Mangosteen — **www.bednbreakfasthomes.com**

MEDEX — **www.medexassist.com**

MedjetAssist — **www.medjetassistance.com**

Ministry of Tourism, India — **www.tourism.gov.in**

Nerd's Eye View — **www.nerdseyeview.com**

Netflix — **www.netflix.com**

No-Jet-Lag — **www.nojetlag.com**

Orbitz — **www.orbitz.com**

Osho Meditation Resort — **www.osho.com**

Pacsafe — **www.pacsafe.com**

Palace on Wheels — **www.palaceonwheels.net**

Passport Canada — **www.ppt.gc.ca**

Playfair Trading — **www.playfairtrading.com**

Servas International — **www.servas.org**

Skype — **www.skype.com**

Sony (Reader Digital Book) — **www.sonystyle.com**

SteriPEN — **www.steripen.com**

TerraPass — **www.terrapass.com**

Time Out — **www.timeout.com**

Transitions Abroad — **www.transitionsabroad.com**

Transportation Security Administration — **www.tsa.gov**

Travisa Outsourcing — **www.indian-visa.com**

U.S. Department of State — **www.iafdb.travel.state.gov**

VolunteerTibet — **www.volunteertibet.org**

Wanderlust and Lipstick — **www.wanderlustandlipstick.com**

Western Union — **www.westernunion.com**

Women on Wanderlust — **www.wowsumitra.com**

World Wide Opportunities on Organic Farms — **www.wwoof.org**

Youth Hostels Association of India — **www.yhaindia.org**

INDEX